Miles D

JAZZ MASTERS SERIES

Miles Davis

BARRY McRAE

Selected Discography by
Tony Middleton

For Ethel and Charles

First published in Great Britain in 1988 by
APOLLO PRESS LIMITED
11 Baptist Gardens, London NW5 4ET

British Library Cataloguing in Publication Data
McRae, Barry
  Miles Davis.—(Jazz masters series; v.14)
  1. Davis, Miles   2. Jazz musicians—
  United States—Biography
  I. Title   II. Middleton, Tony   III. Series
  785.42'092'4   ML419.D39

ISBN 0-948820-05-5

Series editor: David Burnett James

Typesetting by concept Communications, Crayford, Kent

Printed and Bound in Great Britain by
Anchor Brendon Limited, Tiptree, Essex

Contents

Illustrations

Introduction

Miles Davis is a major figure in jazz history. He has been at the forefront of many of its revolutionary changes but his role in them has not always been fully understood. He came to bebop with the thrill of discovery at an early age only to find it dismissed, or worse, by many older musicians and establishment scribes. He was then criticized, while still only a teenager, for failing to match the creative genius of Charlie Parker at the height of his powers.

He was later involved in experiments in sound with Gil Evans, Gerry Mulligan and John Carisi and, although they succeeded aesthetically, they outstripped the listening public by some years. In any real sense, his involvement with this 'cool' jazz was meagre but, by a strange quirk of fate, he was elevated to the status of high priest in a musical religion that was not his.

His problems in the early fifties were many and, not least of these, was a shortage of regular work. It was not until 1955 that he really stamped his personality on jazz, when he formed a quintet that was to have a lasting effect on the music. It introduced John Coltrane to a world that was, for once, ready and it led to a cross fertilisation of ideas between the two men. Davis also renewed his association with Gil Evans and together they produced some of the most memorable works of the era.

Coltrane left and after a reasonable span of time Davis moved off on a similarly stimulating path, this time in the company of tenor saxophonist, Wayne Shorter. It was to be a journey that took Davis dangerously near to his only real failure. Walking precariously in the vanguard was this man's métier, however, and the trumpeter has emerged from the excesses of his rock music fusion into a style that has derived the best from both areas.

The Parker Years

Miles Dewey Davis Jnr. was born in Alton, Illinois, on 25th May 1926. His father was both dentist and landowner and, in the year following the birth of their son, the financially secure Davis family moved to East St. Louis. Within the house, Davis faced the paradox of a racially inhibited mother and a proud and more liberated father. His own life was far from repressed, he made use of the family estate, became a good horseman and generally enjoyed the kind of emotional security that was bound to build his confidence.

Regrettably, East St. Louis was a self-consciously racial city and, at an early age, Davis's domestic security was challenged by red neck extremism. It was a situation complicated by his mother's acceptance of white standards and by her negative attitudes toward black music. Davis was later to discover that she was well able to play blues piano but, during his formative years, her instrument was the violin.

Davis's father, Miles II, felt more pride in his black past. He admired the positive way that his own father, born little more than five years after the Emancipation, had mastered simple accountancy. Miles II also had a taste for jazz and resented the way in which his wife's racial inhibitions coloured her thinking on most subjects. Their mutual antipathy later led them to divorce but, significantly, it was, at least in part, the reason that Miles senior gave his son a trumpet for his thirteenth birthday. Perhaps as a reaction to his wife's attitudes he also chose a teacher, Elwood Buchanan, with strong jazz sympathies.

Elementary musical knowledge was acquired at school and Davis augmented this with his regular lessons and with the aid of a one-

9

dollar Georgia Gibb Chord Book that he had bought for himself. His progress was above average and, by the time he was fifteen, he was playing in his high school band as well as with the Eddie Randall Blue Devils in St. Louis.

It was at this stage of his life that the bearable jibes of racial prejudice took unacceptable and tangible form. Unimportant musical competitions at school were rigged in favour of inferior white pupils and the seeds of Davis's proud aggression were sowed. This fact had no debilitating effect on his instrumental progress, however, and he continued to listen to music from all ethnic sources.

Much has been made of the influences to which Davis may have been exposed. A popular myth has grown up that there is a definitive St. Louis style of trumpet playing. Certainly, lyricists such as Shorty Baker, Joe Thomas and Clark Terry would seem to have had common ties, despite working in different musical areas. Weighed against this, there were declamatory jazzmen like Mouse Randolf and Louis Metcalfe who could just as easily represent a totally different St. Louis style.

The most that can truthfully be said is that the young Davis is more likely to have heard his own townsfolk in his formative years. Clark Terry, five years older than Miles, was the one that he heard most often. Terry has always been suspicious of claims of direct influence but he has said 'I was one of the guys he heard when he was learning'. In fact, Terry was a drinking friend of Buchanan's and, after an initial skirmish with Davis, he became a social companion and a jam session colleague.

It was obvious that the controlled lyricism of Baker and Thomas had a special appeal for Davis and, when his tutor aquainted him with similarly-motivated trumpeters such as Freddie Webster and Bobby Hackett, Davis responded positively. He especially enjoyed the way in which the latter 'stayed around the middle register and, above all, always had something to say'. Davis made 'saying something' his own creed, although his own playing avoided the element of sweetness that occasionally crept into the Webster/ Hackett vocabulary.

The important thing in the life of the young teenager at this time, was that he had now heard altoist Charlie Parker and trumpeter Dizzy Gillespie on record. The lack of sentimentality in the music of these bebop pioneers struck an immediate chord with him and he

10

became determined to get involved. If he was not totally committed to their mode of delivery, he could easily compromise in a style that set such daunting creative standards. His temperament demanded a greater degree of understatement and Terry's brand of bop proposed a pleasing alternative. In the event, Davis never adopted it but at least to the extent of following a lyrical and less convoluted path, he stayed true to the spirit of the St. Louis myth.

In several ways he had prepared unconsciously to turn his back on the 'old ways'. His early training has eschewed all traces of a vibrato from his playing and this gave him the clean sound that became so distinctive. He had developed a tonal quality that was similarly personal and he continued to strive for a 'broad' and full tone. Encouraged by Terry, he began using a Heim mouthpiece and is reputed to have done so ever since. This was ideal for his requirements and Ian Carr, himself a fine trumpeter, explained that this model with its deep cup aided Davis's progress (5). He added that 'it helped in the production of a full sound', although he was at odds to point out that it made it 'more difficult to play high notes'.

Miles did complicate his life at the age of sixteen when he became a shotgun bridegroom. The family were understandably shocked, but life was coming on apace for the young man and he was only eighteen and still a high school senior when he had his first taste of the big time, albeit somewhat briefly. The Billy Eckstine Band came to St. Louis with Gillespie, Parker, Dexter Gordon and Art Blakey in the line-up. Whilst there, trumpeter Buddy Anderson had tuberculosis confirmed and returned to his home in Oklahoma City. Miles Davis, hearing that his idols were in town, turned up at rehearsal and was on hand to fill the gap in the horn section.

By now the family had accepted that their son was going to be a musician and in 1945 he was encouraged to enrol at the Juilliard School of Music in New York. This, in effect, provided parental approval for the less academic activities that Miles had in mind. Although at school during the day, he was determined to spend most of the evenings listening to bebop in clubs, and it was not long before he was taking more seriously the lessons received by this more empirical method.

Being a young man he was not forced to unlearn an already formulated style as had been the case with men like Howard McGhee or Charlie Shavers. He could centralize his thoughts on mastering

11

the new bebop language and he showed considerable wisdom in approaching the problem from both the academic and practical extremes.

On arriving in New York Davis had, at first, found difficulty in locating Charlie Parker but it was not long before he was playing with him at The Three Deuces on 52nd Street. The altoist was the perfect model. Here was the man who had extended jazz on three fronts. At the heart of his style, he had ushered jazz away from simple, melodic improvisation. He rebuilt elaborate new tunes on established chord sequences and made them formal structures in their own right. His timing was equally revolutionary. Playing through bar lines and placing notes in an off-centre manner was hardly unknown, but Parker's angular approach brought a new dimension to note displacement. Finally, there was the sound he brought to the instrument. His tone had a far harder edge than the swing era altoists and he delivered his solos with an emotional force that took it an inestimable distance from the jazz romantics.

These changes did not come about overnight, nor were they the work of a single hand, but they came together in Parker and he was the man that Davis turned to as mentor. In one sense the fact that he was a saxophonist rather than a trumpeter was a disadvantage. There could be none of the musician's intimacies – what mouthpiece to use – what embouchure or what fingering to employ. What Parker and Davis came to have was a leader – sideman relationship based on a mutual respect that certain observers at the time were less than willing to confirm.

Jazz has a history of stylistic leaders on one instrument inspiring others to apply the new discoveries to another. Trumpeter Louis Armstrong's influence on pianist Earl Hines and trombonist Jimmy Harrison were obvious examples but, in more recent years, altoist Ornette Coleman was the keystone on which the free form players on almost every instrument built their styles. Parker's influence was equally widespread in the forties and this was acknowledged with due humour when bassist Charles Mingus wrote *'If Charlie Parker Were A Gunslinger There'd Be A Whole Lot Of Dead Copycats'*.

Even for the more imaginative, however, it was an important starting point and Davis was indeed fortunate to get his 'instruction' first hand and at a time when the great altoist was at the height of his powers. Playing on 52nd also brought him into direct contact with men like Gillespie, Bud Powell, Coleman Hawkins and Thelonious Monk, something which raised his standing with his peers and directed him on the fastest route to professional competence as a jazz musician. His appetite for the new music knew no limits and during 1946 he actually languished in the trumpet section of the Benny Carter Band, just to be on the West Coast near to his idols.

It was not a one way affair, though, because Parker had begun to speak glowingly of his somewhat sycophantic shadow. So much so that he was now prepared to extend the invitation of a record date. Gillespie and Parker had encouraged Davis to try New York after the Eckstine meeting but now it was the altoist, with an ideal line-up and a record date for Savoy, who had chosen the young trumpeter when other men were available.

In the event, the date was not without its disasters. Pianist Thelonious Monk failed to turn up and Argonne Thornton (later known as Sadik Hakim) was called in to deputize. Although Thornton had been working out of Chicago and Peoria, he had been in New York for some months and had a more than passing acquaintance with the new music. Whether Gillespie was intended for the gig in addition to Davis has never been completely clarified but, in any case, he had just signed a contract with Musicraft and appeared incognito. To cap matters, Parker experienced reed trouble in the warm up and left the studio for a midtown music shop.

Finally, it got under way and there was Davis recording at last with his own bebop guru. Whether Parker chose Davis because he liked his strangely (at the time) static playing and self-effacing musical modesty, we will never know. Ross Russell (10) claimed that Parker had said he did not want 'a virtuoso capable of fireworks' but rather a man 'who played a relaxed legato style, with a warm tone, in the lower and middle registers'. This does smack of someone fitting words to suit the case, although the way in which Davis was used in his solo and ensemble parts, does suggest that his leader had certain strong views about his role. It was most probably that Parker saw no harm in having a bandsman, presenting little serious challange to his solo supremacy, still somewhat limited instrumentally, but one he hoped could perform the straight forward charts with dedicated competence.

Certainly, Davis was not a new superstar to compare with Parker, Gillespie and Bud Powell, but neither was he the incompetent that opponents of bop claimed at the time. Savoy declared the date to be the 'Greatest Recording Session In Modern Jazz History' and, in the sense that it was the first to present a purpose-built bebop quintet without stylistic outsiders, they were probably justified at that time.

With the precedent set it was only a matter of time before another label, in this case Dial, got in on the act. Ross Russell formed it to specialize in bebop and Parker's small band was the most obvious target.

The first recording session took place in Hollywood in March 1946 and it exhibited the same element of chaos as had the Savoy date. Parker reshuffled his personnel shortly before the event and then turned up on the day with nothing written. Themes had to be learnt on the spot and 'head' arrangements worked out as the group went along. In retrospect, it can be seen as an important lesson for Davis, one that showed just what could be achieved with almost incontinent freedom.

Things had not worked out as Davis would have liked in California, however, and after leaving Benny Carter to join Parker, he found the club in which they worked closed without warning. Strangely, it was again the Billy Eckstine Band that played an important part in his salvation. Davis rejoined the band in Los Angeles and used it as a means to return east.

Parker, for his part, had been in trouble. His drug addiction had brought him to the brink of insanity and he had been admitted to the Camarillo State Hospital. His seven-month stay at that institution ended in April 1947, but he had returned to New York and within days he had a band in rehearsal for a booking at the Three Deuces Club. The quintet comprised Parker, Davis, pianist Duke Jordan, bassist Tommy Potter and drummer Max Roach and they were to remain together for something like twenty months. The four week stay was extended indefinitely and, although they played 'away' for specific engagements, they were on hand to make a remarkable series of records for both Savoy and Dial.

Occasionally, the odd outsider was called in to deputise but this was the group that was rightly regarded as the 'combo of the day'. Such has been the interest in their music that their output has been the subject of a strategic re-issue programme in which, not only were the accepted titles put out, but also rejected takes and parts of rejected takes. Because of this, we have been able to examine the

14

evolving process of improvisation and to see how these men worked out their musical problems as they went along.

The playing of Miles Davis, on these sessions, has always evoked mixed reactions, but it would be totally unfair if, before discussing it, the whole situation was not put into perspective. Here was a man, barely twenty, from a good, middle class home and fired with perhaps an unhealthy degree of idealism. He found himself with a difficult leader, one whom he worshipped musically and one who complicated the relationship by liking his young associate and by sensing a potential in his still slightly inchoate work.

It cannot be denied, that there was a degree of uncertainty in his work but, as yet, the ground rules for the bop quintet trumpeter had not been laid down. Only Dizzy Gillespie and Fats Navarro had shown the ability to match the more readily fluent saxophone lead in tight unisons, to produce the clearly articulated delivery with minimal use of vibrato and achieve the brassy, tonal quality that lent the urgent edge so vital to bop. In fact, what Davis was doing was building from these standards and arriving at a less idiosyncratic style and one that could act as a guide to those that followed. It was still not an easy path and it is hard to think of any brass men who avoided difficulties with the style in their early years. Excellent swing era converts like Charlie Shavers and Howard McGhee, never quite mastered the art and even trumpeters of the calibre of Lee Morgan, Freddie Hubbard and Donald Byrd struggled in their very earliest recording dates. One cannot even exclude Clifford Brown from this observation; the demands of bebop were considerable and it was Davis who best answered them.

Inevitably, at recording sessions, Charlie Parker was enpowered to choose the 'take' that was to be used. He usually waited until he was satisfied, so it became almost traditional that he chose the last cut. Obviously some first attempts were so pleasing that further takes were superfluous, although it is significant from the standpoint of this book that Parker's choice was nearly always made on the accuracy with which the theme statements were presented and on the quality of his own personal solos. This meant that, but for the re-issue programme, some of the better trumpet solos might not have been heard.

Weighed against this, Ross Russell reported that, at the first Dial session, Davis was 'not playing much in his solos but was warming the ensemble parts with his broad tone'. He also added that 'the mistakes were in all cases the fault of the sidemen'. With this in mind, it is surprising that the trumpet work is at least acceptable and in certain cases quite outstanding and, on the strength of even the early titles, Davis went on to win *Down Beat's* New Star award in 1946. It is also on record that, when picking the Three Deuces band, Parker had said that Davis was his 'first and only choice' on trumpet.

The critical mistake made by some observers is to judge the Savoy and Dial sessions as if they were all the same. Davis played very differently in the two year span that embraced them and it is not unreasonable to use them to monitor his progress. On the November 1946 date, when Davis's nerves really showed, there were parts that he would not even attempt. To make matters worse, his solos were an uneasy compromise between Freddie Webster's bigger tone and Dizzy Gillespie's phraseology.

On the March 1946 session he was far more confident, although he rarely seemed able to sustain the fluency or the mood that he created in his opening phrases. Solos began with a well worked paraphrase of the melody or a pick-up from the previous statement and then lost momentum as he progressed through a parade of favourite phrases. Gillespie remained the lodestar and Davis sounded as if he had prepared the opening of each solo but not thought out the remainder.

Perhaps the presence of pianist Bud Powell changed the climate for the session in the May of the following year. Certainly Gillespie seemed a less pervading influence, but it was not a happy date for the young trumpeter. His timing was often stilted and there remained a maladroitness about his solo organisation that left it unbalanced. The August date corrected that particular fault and it could well be that this was because he had written all of the material used. It meant that he knew the bare bones of each theme and he gave his followers their first real glimpse of the Davis musical précis.

All led logically to the Dial sessions at the end of 1947. By this time, the quintet had been working together consistently and Davis was in excellent form. He had largely escaped the stylistic extremes of the bebop trumpeters and had turned instead toward the more spatially aware saxophone players or even toward the older St. Louis trumpeters. It seems impossible that Davis could introduce gentle almost reflective moods into the turmoil of bop, but this he did. Most especially it was on the slower pieces, and titles like *Embraceable You*, *Out Of Nowhere* and *My Old Flame* point the way to the time when Davis solos would be judged as 'metamorphoses' rather than 'variations on a theme'.

Capitol Gains

During 1947 Davis had met arranger Gil Evans when the Canadian pianist sought a release on *Donna Lee*, Davis's brilliant *Indiana* variation. This had been granted and the tune was subsequently recorded by the Claude Thornhill Band with some success. More significantly, it led to Davis studying some of Evans's scores and becoming interested in the music of this unusual band.

In the following year their friendship flourished and Davis joined a small coterie of musicians meeting in Evans's apartment, in the main to discuss the possibilities of this unique style. Pianist John Lewis and baritone saxophonist Gerry Mulligan were among the number and between them they set out to create a jazz equivalent of the Thornhill Band with as few musicians as they could manage.

Evans always maintained that Thornhill, himself an arranger, had evolved the band 'sound'. The leader had scored trombones with woodwinds and had already added french horns in 1941, the year that Evans joined. The horns were merged effortlessly with brass and reeds and the idea of sectional interplay completely abandoned. Evans spoke of a 'characteristic voicing for the Thornhill Band as a french horn lead, one or sometimes two french horns playing in unison or a duet. . . . The clarinet doubled the melody, also playing lead. Below were two altos, a tenor and a baritone or two altos and two tenors'. (1).

Thornhill, personally, played in a style not too distant from that of Teddy Wilson and what Evans introduced in the post-war years was the improvisational notion of bebop into the band's formal setting.

18

Strangely enough, it was not too violent a meeting and on *Anthropology* there was even some Wilsonesque piano before the Thornhill voiced- Gill Evans-shaped arrangement appeared. Similarly, *Donna Lee* had its own idiosyncracies with muted trumpets and reeds scored in D flat! An effect that, on record, came over almost as if playing a slower piece at the wrong speed.

In 1948 Gerry Mulligan joined Thornhill and by this time the band had added a tuba to the roster of melody instruments. Most of the really distinctive arrangements were coming from Evans, and Mulligan admitted that the Canadian was instrumental in his re-thinking much of what he had previously held sacrosanct in the arranging art. They were charts that convinced him that he 'wanted to play his idiom within that kind of sound' and, when Davis offered him the chance to do so, he quit Thornhill.

By 1948 Davis had left Parker and had also deserted 52nd Street. He had made a base at New York's Royal Roost and, with pianist Tadd Dameron, was leading a group that included trombonist Kai Winding and tenor saxophonist Allen Eager. Davis somehow managed to persuade the Roost to take on another band, and he took in his cohorts from Evans's apartment, the men who were investigating the new sound. A recording ban had just ended and, even more surprisingly, Davis induced Capitol to record them.

In the event, the band played for only two weeks at the Club. Audience reaction was negative and the band's option was not renewed. There were two broadcasts and a short residency at the Clique Club in the following year but, apart from a few perceptive critics and fellow musicians, there was little support for the band.

Fortunately for posterity, recordings from the 'Metropolitan Bopera House' were unearthed in the seventies and they gave a real insight into the band's performances. Compared with the later recordings they were more hectic, and could be said to lack the unforced grace of the studio versions. They did include two items not used by Capitol, but these were in the same mould and show the genuine spirit of the band.

In fairness, the band and its achievements are best judged by the three recording sessions that took place in 1949 and 1950. For them the selection of the personnel was a challenge and, on balance, Davis chose wisely. The rhythm section had a very specialized role and it was never in less than good hands. On the piano stool for the first session sat the redoubtable Al Haig and he surrendered it for the remainder to John Lewis. Two extrovert drummers held down that difficult job, although Roach, on the first and third dates, and Kenny Clarke subjugated their more aggressive personalities for the general good. Three bassists were used and although Joe Schulman, Al McKibbon and Nelson Boyd are hardly taxed, all acquitted themselves well.

Kai Winding's clipped and slightly regimented trombone on session one was replaced by the smoother, more legato talents of J.J. Johnson on the rest, while the formalised french horn parts were despatched by three highly competent musicians in Junior Collins, Gunther Schuller and Sandy Siegelstein. Only the tuba of John Barber, the baritone of Gerry Mulligan, the alto of Lee Konitz and the leader's trumpet were ever present.

Superficially, the various recorded titles had a similarity, but this was more a question of mood. With an ensemble range of three and a half octaves available, the various arrangers found no difficulty in giving each selection a personality of its own. On the first recording date in January 1949, *Move*, although arranged by John Lewis, came over as something of a jam session piece. On *Godchild*, in contrast, arranger Gerry Mulligan took advantage of the tonal depth at his disposal and from a tuba led opening, allowed Davis's solo to rise like a phoenix from the lower reaches of the ensemble fire. It was, in effect a very good solo and probably one of his best in the series. It filled a relaxed thirty two bars, was well landscaped and had a natural lyricism that spoke of a growing confidence. His solo on Mulligan's *Jeru* just failed to match it for fluency, yet ironically this was a very smooth chart, obviously the work of a saxophonist and one that offered the kind of well rounded, melodic contours that are comfortable for any instrumentalist.

In fact, it is rather difficult to describe the group's overall sound in words. For all its tonal depth, it had a light almost floating feeling, a textural quality that moved the listener through musical shadows of varying densities. As such, it suited Davis very well. There was not the challenge of a Parker, he was not required to play high notes, nor was he asked to sustain long, melodic lines. The ensemble panoply covered his every move without overpowering it, and subdued 'organ chords' were a cushion on which Davis languished stylishly.

Davis actually carried the lead, at least in part, on many of the titles and he did so with the assurance of an old fashioned first trumpet. On Mulligan's *Venus De Milo* his lead became a solo with seamless ease and the natural transition virtually carried him into a restrained and correspondingly coherent exposition. The virtues of the old style trumpet stations are again invoked on *Israel*, probably the most orthodox arrangement of the series. Davis and Konitz solo in the normal manner but, although arranger John Carisi maintains the Capitol band voicing, there is something of the swing era call and response formula about the chart.

French critic André Hodier once claimed, with some justification, that *Boplicity* alone was 'enough to qualify Gil Evans as one of jazz's greatest arranger-composers'. Yet somehow it is *Moon Dreams* that seems to typify the music of the whole project. It contains no full lengths solos but seems, more than any other, to draw attention to the size of the band. It is a masterpiece of scoring and makes obvious that this is the minimum line-up of instruments that could possibly be used to achieve this depth of sound and breadth of expression. Toward its end, a canon is worked in reverse to remind us of the mechanics of making music, but this is an ensemble triumph and will always be judged as such.

How then should we judge the entire Capitol project? Commercially it was a disaster and it would be easy to take the esoteric stance and pity the unknowing. Yet, outstanding music was produced and a genuine attempt was made to broaden jazz horizons. *Jazz* audiences do have an instinct for the real thing, however, and we must, at least, acknowledge their rejection of the result. A more balanced view can be made by simply looking at the music's strengths and weaknesses in terms of jazz made before, and with advantage of hindsight, that which has come since.

To see the band as the torch bearers of the 'cool' school is an oversimplification and one that does the band no credit. The Capitol band put only limited emphasis on solos and apart from Davis, who played his individual statements rather well, the standard of soloing was not high. In view of his later achievements, Mulligan's efforts were particularly pedestrian, and only Konitz's varied solo on *Rouge* came anywhere near to the quality of his subsequent work.

The cool school had its bigger bands, but they had different aims and it became an era of jazz history best remembered for the solo artistry of men like Art Pepper, Bud Shank, Chet Baker, Stan Getz and Gerry Mulligan. The Capitol band, in complete contrast, put its faith in its collective strength, its arrangers were the 'soloists', the men set to express themselves in an individual way, and each composition became a separate entity because of the way in which its performance was realised. True, most were comparatively static in conception but this was intentional and all of the arrangers involved were cognizant of the technical limitation of the leader.

The extent of their success and the reason that this shared musical experience had validity, is that they managed to accommodate Davis at this stage of his career, not by diminishing him as a jazzman but actually by presenting him in a perfect setting. It was one that could actually have launched him into the next stage of his career had circumstances not temporarily arrested his development.

Keeping the Wheels on

In practice, what had happened is that the Capitols had established Davis as a leader. He now faced the frustrations of job hustling in New York without the clear stylistic identity that the nonet gave him and without the dominating influence of Parker. For his own part, he was still enamoured with the idea of presenting his skills in a big band context and toward the end of 1949, with the second set of Capitol recordings as yet unmade, he rehearsed a big band with Tadd Dameron. The personnel included Red Rodney, Bernie Glow, Zoot Sims, Allen Eager, Cecil Payne, Kai Winding, Matthew Gee and Shadow Wilson, but it was an idea that failed.

Even established big bands of the period were finding it difficult to work, and Davis could find nobody willing to take a chance with an esoteric new unit. He took the most obvious alternative and returned to the vagaries of leading a small combo in the New York club world of the time.

To complicate matters he had just experienced the culture shock of his first visit across the Atlantic. The parochial European jazz world was locked in a futile stylistic war and Davis had been used as a tool for the moderns. The treatment he received was unctuous in the extreme and a return to New York brought him sharply back to the realities of the 'jazz jungle'.

Until this time he had remained aloof from the drug use of the bebop generation. His dedication to his music, perhaps even more than his middle class background, had led him to ignore rather than resist it. The combined frustrations of public rejection, a mixed media reaction and the lack of regular work, changed his attitude.

Like many before him he embarked on a course of revenge that took him rapidly towards self destruction. In a very short time he became a heroin addict and, with his father's allowance to rely on, he was able to afford the more modest prices of the time.

A further complication was that the volatile American jazz world was again moving on a different tack. The change was more gradual than in the preceeding five years, but it represented a strong change in musical emphasis. A perhaps unnatural importance was placed on 'restraint' and, ironically, Davis was seen as the Messiah of 'Cool' jazz. In retrospect, the position is clearer. The change of emphasis that took place did so on the West Coast, in the main amongst a collection of white musicians who had tailored the music of the bebop masters to their own needs. Much of it was jazz of good quality but it was, in most cases, some distance from the style of Davis. The trumpeter had always insisted that he wanted a light sound and the legato movement of the Capitol band had accommodated that to perfection. It was not a 'cool' sound in the true sense, however, and critic Alun Morgan perhaps came nearest to sensing the difference by describing his playing as exhibiting the 'Modern Hackett' approach (*Jazz Journal* Nov. 1953).

Certainly the inner warmth of that Dixielander's style can be compared with Davis, and both men were masters of the well-designed phrase. Perhaps where they differed, at that time, was in terms of technique. It was in this area that Davis still had his shortcomings. His range remained a barrier to certain areas of improvisation and his new life style was hardly an aid to the arduous demands of trumpet playing. The growing confidence seen and heard during his last year with Parker was arrested and too often there were ill-formed notes to speak of instrumental uncertainty.

Weighed against this, his tone had acquired a well ripened maturity, a quality that made it easily recognised. In a blind-fold test in France's *Jazz Magazine* (April 1955), Dizzy Gillespie actually mistook him for Clifford Brown but one would have normally identified the Davis sound with ease.

Unfortunately, scuffling for heroin was having a serious effect on his music and for some time he left New York completely. A shortage of money had become a problem and he was playing neither well nor often. Ironically, he won the *Metronome* trumpet poll in the years 1951, '52 and '53, although it is probable that he would regard that fact with some cynicism in the light of subsequent achievements.

Fortunately, he did get some recording opportunities, but the early fifties were not a period of musical triumph for Davis. Moments of inspiration and passages of flaccid stagnation were too often bed fellows and Whitney Balliett summed it up succinctly (2) when he said that 'Davis' slow playing is a calculated lisping, an attack of hesitancy and discreet forward rushes. One no longer looks for perfect solos but for spots and passages that stand as miniature perfections'.

What is not always acknowledged is that it was a period which saw a realignment of his ideals. The ever present shadow cast by Dizzy Gillespie over his earlier efforts had now faded. Davis had accommodated the bebop style within his own ethic, although to do so he had, to some extent, lost sight of his roots. The influence of the white players involved in the Capitol venture had concentrated his thinking on improvisation at the expense of all other jazz considerations and had left him uncertain of his aims.

This was a problem that resolved itself as Davis, by choice of personnel, moved slowly away from the cooler aspects of his style. His health problem did not help, but in his best moments he was a lucid and imaginative jazzman. With his finances still a problem he occasionally accepted club dates and recording sessions as a sideman, although on these his contribution was often less than adequate and he remained strongly affected by the company in which he found himself.

He made one recording date with the New York wing of the cool school. The leader on that ocasion was Lee Konitz, although one must conjecture as to his motives for using Davis as his trumpeter. The classic records of his mentor Lennie Tristano had avoided the use of trumpet and, although Davis would seem the only choice, it represented quite a departure.

The term 'Third Stream', a music to fill that nebulous area between European Classical and Jazz, was being used to describe the Tristano work. It was no more accurate for Tristano than it would have been to describe the Davis Capitols, and it proved to be a rather pointless red herring. In the event, the session was far from successful. Davis sounded diffident and the music, with its strategic use of spaces, left him naked at a time when he was less able to accept the glare of the spotlight.

It actually sounds as if Davis's heart was never in these performances at all, as if he and the group were ill prepared. Certainly he made no attempt to play the difficult *Ezz-thetic* theme. Konitz took it as a lead and the trumpeter noodled a contrapuntal support part. In fact, it worked rather well but it did lend credence to the theory that Davis had not prepared to play the real part.

One almost senses that Davis had enough on his plate, just making a living and staying alive, to worry about the long term reaction of critics or of posterity's analysis of his work in the troubled early 1950's. This apparent apathy did not extend to his fellow musicians, however, and one partnership that he encouraged was that with Sonny Rollins. Still only twenty-one when he joined Davis's working combo in 1951, the young tenor man responded and over the next five years made recordings that were an unofficial progress report of a jazzman's growth from rookie to seasoned campaigner.

Unfortunately, their earliest efforts did not see the best of either man, even if the widely experienced Davis should have shown better. A broody, feeling blues was predictably Davis's most outstanding contribution to their first recording session, but his excellently redesigned *Whispering* is totally undermined by bad execution and on *Blue Room* he plays like a nervous beginner. Years later it still rankled and he pulled up Alun Morgan with a 'Hell man, I was playing badly on that date. I was . . . you know'.

The real point is that Rollins, for all his earliest limitations, represented a more earthy approach, one that Davis equated with his own return to stylistic base. Later that year, things got better for Davis, at least, and comparison with the October's *My Old Flame* and the Dial version of 1947 tells the listener of both Davis's development and of his change of attitudes. In the earlier example he came in with an introduction, obviously worked out in advance. In fact, he made it quite brilliantly and then proceeded to fashion a solo of tidy but ordinary dimensions. On the 1951 session he began less ambitiously and, with the gauntlet still firmly in his grasp, he courted the *Old Flame* with soft words rather than flamboyant passion. Odd notes were still cracked but the desire to let the solo take its own pace, made for a more balanced result.

Davis's musical relationship with Parker could be the subject of a

26

book in itself but it is instructive to examine a situation in which roles are reversed. Even when he himself was leader, the trumpeter seems reluctant to take full control and, on a Prestige date early in 1953 one could almost suspect Davis of attempting to imbue his work with an artificial gaiety. It was as if he wanted to convince Parker that all was right in his own world.

Fortunately, Davis had almost reached the corner and, although his work in 1954 did not equal that of the immediately subsequent years, it had begun to re-establish him as a major soloist and as a gifted jazz musician. He did not become a virtuoso overnight, indeed he has never become one. He did, however, exhibit a growing confidence in most musical situations. A particularly successful 1953 Prestige date, with saxophonists Al Cohn and Zoot Sims, had perhaps hinted at this growing confidence and at clearer, musical thinking, although this was offset by a later date with the seemingly ideal support of John Lewis, Percy Heath and Max Roach, that completely failed to take off.

Certainly, he was no longer overawed by men he might have once deemed superior, nor was he thrown by players less able to compete on equal musical terms. He seemed to be at ease with most people and sessions with men such as Horace Silver and Art Blakey jelled at once. With those worthies he tended to play on their strengths, he kept to medium tempos, stayed with his own middle register and let the music take its course.

Blakey's reaction to Davis is significant in view of the drummer's amazing ability to discover trumpet players. He found that 'Miles was cool as a leader – you just played what you wanted. I never considered Miles a great *trumpet* player. I considered him a stylist. He wasn't my idea of a trumpet player like Clifford, Fats (Navarro) or Dizzy, not that kind of power. But whatever he had, he sure used it all. Miles could take a bazooka, and he'd *still* sound the same. He's something else. Beautiful'.

Being the stylist that he undoubtedly was, Davis began to exert his own influence on other players and to inspire and encourage younger men. The Lewis, Heath and Roach team was his working rhythm section, but it was significant that his choice of horn partners included much lesser known figures. Little has been heard of saxophonist David Schildkraut since his heady days with Davis, yet he briefly completed a front line partnership that presented an intriguing contrast. They young altoist played well but clung to the Parkerisms that made him comfortable. Davis showed no inclination to return to this area and, although happy with his strongly bop orientated sideman, played as he might have done with just his backing trio.

His concern for structure within a solo was increasingly evident, but a return to good execution had now begun to enhance all his performances. The Davis trumpet that totally dominated *You Don't Know What Love Is* offered further evidence of his move away from the angular drama of bop and, even more, from the climax building of jazz's earlier eras. The solo took the form of an almost consciously anti-climactic process and literally faded into its conclusion: it could be seen as the trumpeter going further along the line of capturing something of saxophonist Lester Young's airy, vibrato-less method.

Much has been made of the Prez's influence on an army of tenor saxophonists but, in this rich period of Davis's development, the trumpeter came nearer to the total spirit of the Missourian than any reed player. It was not that he designed his solo in the same manner, nor even that he introduced phrases that might have had the Young stamp. It was rather that he traded in similar innuendos, allowed a development to grow gradually and delivered his ideas with the same unhurried blandness that highlighted melodic ingenuity rather than tonal brilliance. The effect for the listener was akin to moving into a cubist canvas by Georges Braque: there was an almost arid quality about the sound texture but there was a three dimensional element that gave each solo a genuine feeling of depth.

Superficial observers explained away the intrinsic beauty of the style by claiming that Davis's delivery was given an element of mystery by his use of mutes. This overlooks the large number of performances, both live and on record, that did not use a mute.

To take the matter a stage further, some were not even made on his own horn. There is the story told by Jules Colomby, a jazz fan who was helping out at Prestige. Davis had turned up at Rudy Van Gelder's studio with J.J. Johnson, Lucky Thompson, but with no horn. At this stage Colomby helped by announcing that he had a trumpet in the trunk of his car. It was an old Buescher he had owned since he was thirteen and it was full of leaks. He wondered how Davies was going to be able to play it at all but then related how 'Miles warmed up by just going over the valves with his fingers, to see if they were loose. Then he counted off the tempo to *Walkin'* without saying a word. It was just a blues, and everyone knew the tune'.

For Davis it turned out to be an important landmark. As an entire extended play release and as one side of a long playing album it enjoyed considerable commercial success and for the first time in some years the trumpeter's career was again up and running.

It was not all plain sailing, however, and later in the year he had a traumatic experience as he crossed swords on a record date with the daunting Thelonious Monk. In view of Davis's success with the pianist's compositions, it should have been a labour of love. In effect, it was a disaster and created a rift between the two men that was never to be healed.

Alun Morgan (3) described it as an argumentative chip-on-the-shoulder affair: 'clashes of temperament brought the atmosphere to fever pitch and Davis is said to have refused to play his solo if Monk accompanied him.' Davis certainly sounded at home with Heath's walking bass alternative but, despite this, Monk did not comply with the leader's instructions and, in the event, comped with some sensitivity behind Davis's assertive opening solo on the session's last take, *The Man I Love*. In actual fact, the whole session proved to be successful for Davis and in all of this turmoil two important things occurred. Firstly, we had the occasional (enforced) laying-out of the pianist, a device that Davis was later to employ more strategically. Secondly we had, on *Swing Spring*, the soloists working from a scale instead of a chord sequence. Greater freedom was immediately available and it certainly acted as a pointer to detailed experiments in this direction that were just around the corner.

The significant point was that Davis was now a jazzman of stature and the men he worked with had to compete on his terms. The Miles Davis stylistic die had been cast, but it was one that could accept surprisingly different compounds and still turn out a finished product with the trumpeter's unmistakeable stamp. One would be pushed to imagine a more incongruous line-up than one including former big band men like trombonist Britt Woodman and vibraphonist Teddy Charles, bass playing maverick Charles Mingus and drummer Elvin Jones from the boiler house of Detroit hard bop.

This was a group that did succeed, however, and in its one Debut recording date it used the Davis language but with a vernacular of its own. The ringing, strangely funereal tones of Charles's vibes were an ideal match for the trumpeter's doomy, muted mood and a simple development of a theme like *Nature Boy* spoke of an inherent honesty, not of a limitation.

Obviously a Davis working with such a group would not have the elasticity of support that his roster of early fifties pianists had provided. John Lewis, Horace Silver, Ray Bryant and newcomer Red Garland all had a trace of 'old style' swing in their playing and this had given Davis buoyancy even in his most tortuous expositions.

What perhaps distinguished the next and most vital part of his career was that Davis, a newly established master of his harmonic and melodic directions, began to develop the rhythmic side of his music to an equal extent. Distorted claims had been made about the influence exerted by the Capitols but it was the formation of his next group that really saw him consolidate his move from the role of the influenced to that of the influencer.

The most important thing, however, was that Davis kicked his drug habit at the beginning of 1954. In the event, he did so in a manner compatible with his former middle class resolve. He sought neither medical or psychiatric assistance but merely took himself off, and alone endured the horrors of 'cold turkey'. It was a nightmare of solitary sickness and near starvation but it opened the door to a new future and a period of unparalleled musical success.

If the Crown Fits

A gain in confidence was an indisputable factor in the change that took place in Davis and his music, and this came about more due to an adjustment in mental attitude than to some amazing change in his instrumental powers. It has been acknowledged that he never became a virtuoso but this was the ultimate coming together of head, lips and hands, the realisation that a player must have enough technique to deliver, in terms of sounds, all that his head hears.

The advancements of 1954 were consolidated on all fronts in 1955. Davis's health was not entirely good but he had begun to take seriously the business of keeping fit. He had enjoyed a personal triumph at the Newport Jazz Festival and had begun piecing together one of the best bands he was ever to lead. Red Garland and Philly Joe Jones were the first to join. Garland was a composite of several pianists who had worked for Davis in the recent past and Jones was the drummer that gave Davis the fire he wanted. Close behind came bassist Paul Chambers, a product of the Detroit hard bop school and still only twenty.

Originally, Davis had thought he would like Sonny Rollins to complete his line-up, but the enigmatic tenor saxophonist, had gone to Chicago for one of his sabbaticals and had been reluctant to return to New York. There were several alternatives but finally Davis settled for John Coltrane. Jones, a fellow Philadephian, strongly recommended him and Davis, remembering a meeting some years before, hired him.

As a collective unit it was untried and not everybody was convinced of its potential. In his honest and perceptive sleeve notes for the album *Steamin'* Joe Goldberg described the new group, *the* Miles Davis Quintet (including John Coltrane, Red Garland, Paul Chambers and Philly Joe Jones) with an unerring and rather daunting realism: 'The group consisted, we are told, of a trumpet player who could play only in the middle register and fluffed half his notes; an out-of-tune tenor player; a cocktail pianist; a drummer who played so loud that no one else could be heard; and a teenage bassist'.

This was some indictment and it was not without its grains of truth. One would be doing Davis less than justice if his early problems with the group were ignored and a parallel might well be drawn with the very earliest Count Basie band; a group with more potential than polish, and another that had to get basic musical and stylistic qualitites right before reaching its full power.

There were other problems, however, and it was not long before the quintet became known on the street, and to bookers, as the 'D and D Band'. This was the 'drunk and dope band' because, although the leader had conquered his own addiction in 1954, he was the only member of the band who was 'clean'.

J.C. Thomas pointed out (4) that 'the constant presence of the "Big H" didn't seem to unduly affect the music', but he did concede that Davis was 'taciturn to the point of diffidence, most of the time, and on other occasions abrasive to the extreme of arousing personal hostility'. The trumpeter was in the position of the reformed smoker. His colleagues were an inevitable clique of users and his coming to terms with the situation went a long way to explaining his 'detached' reputation.

It was certainly not an ideal situation and what Davis had to do was to marshall the talents of this ostensibly incompatible collection of musicians. He had just signed a long term contract to work at Birdland, and the stability that this gave him was a distinct advantage. Wisely he approached the horns and the rhythm section as separate problems and, although this led him into a 'one rule for you, one for me' position, it did work.

The limitations in his own playing he had now turned into a virtue. He set the climate of performace around his own middle register, and it turned out to be a move that found an aesthetic affinity with Coltrane's mat-toned tenor. He encouraged a situation in which both men could grow artistically, and could build on styles that had grown from the roots of bebop. Both he and Trane showed a restlessness about their playing and there was plenty of ill-founded and destructive criticism to discourage them at the time.

The problems facing the rhythm section looked, superficially, more acute. In reality they were overcome with greater ease. Jones's pre-occupation with fortissimo was easily rectified by the use of throttle and in retrospect this was applied with restraint. The style demanded aggressive drum parts and once Davis had balanced his rhythm team, Jones was free to add just what light and dark shading he desired.

The teenage bassist's role was, in some ways, more obviously pre-determined. He was a straight ahead player, not concerned with elaborate flights of fancy, and his playing was ideally suited to Davis's ideal of 'loosening up' his rhythmic base. He seemed able to detach himself from pianist Garland's more obvious accent points and to construct lines that accepted their own contrapuntal responsibilities. One has only to listen to his work behind Davis's solo on tracks such as *S'posin* to hear how, in melodic terms, there is an interaction between bass and trumpet, one achieved almost independently of their other colleagues.

This notwithstanding, there was a true feeling of integration in this rhythm section. Paul Scanlon of *Rolling Stone* (sleeve note of *Workin' and Steamin'*) perhaps slightly overstated the case when he saw them as a trio in their own right. Only once, on *Ahmad's Blues*, did they actually record alone and it is significant that Garland, on his many independent trio recordings, ignored Jones and filled the drum chair with Art Taylor or Charlie Persip.

With the Davis quintet, they had a part to play, and they executed it with panache. Ironically, it was the 'cocktail pianist' who was the most distinctive. He had worked as backing pianist to such vastly different singers as Lips Page and Billy Eckstine. He had also spent some time in the group of romantic tenor saxophonist Ben Webster. With Davis he extended this role of accompanist; the phrase shapes were conceivably too rounded for the cut of the music, but the listener becomes increasingly aware that it was not the melodic fripperies that constituted the style but the firmly wrought block chords that were the essence of this method. These 'singer's signposts' were at the heart of the quintet to such an extent that, even when he laid out, there remained the same element of progression.

Asking his pianist to drop out temporarily was a device that Davis began to exploit with increasing skill and it was one that was to work well in later bands. It did not mean that the rhythm section was not working as a single unit, but rather that certain freer, musical passages could breath more easily without the constraints that might be there, because of the piano's exact diatonic disciplines.

As a tool, it would not have proved effective had not both bassist and drummer grasped the full implications of it. This they did and, as with their normal rhythm section roles, they maintained their own brand of propulsive urgency.

It was as a total unit, however, that the three men scored most effectively. They created a sense of latent, rhythmic power, a feeling that they were only just holding themselves in check. Because of this and because of the direction in which Davis's music was travelling, it worked. Three quite disparate stylists provided just the parts that were needed. Nevertheless, it was not this innovatory rhythm team that made it such an important group. It was Davis's forward looking musical policy, his own brilliant trumpet playing and the rapid emergence of John Coltrane as a major jazz soloist. The enormous contribution to jazz made by the saxophonist is well documented elsewhere but his importance to Davis at the time cannot be over-estimated. To begin with it endorsed the trumpeter's good taste, powers of musical perception and steadfastness in the face of critics.

Musicians with reliable ears have confirmed Coltrane's wayward intonation in his early days but work under the leadership of steadfast professionals like Dizzy Gillespie and Johnny Hodges had ironed out this problem. By 1955, when he first went on record with Miles Davis, it was a thing of the past. What was evident was the individuality of his sound and the unique way in which he placed his notes. Even in the most dense of semi-quaver outbursts there was an intriguing off-centre quality to his timing and a linear insight that made him a perfect foil for his leader.

Davis's faith in his star sideman did not mean, however, that all was plain sailing between them. Both musically and emotionally there were problems and Coltrane said of Davis (4), 'After I joined Miles in 1955 I found that he doesn't talk much and will rarely discuss his music. He is completely unpredictable; sometimes he'd walk off the stage after just a few notes, not even completing one chorus. If I asked him something about his music I never knew how he was going to take it.'

Nevertheless, Davis exploited their musical contrasts and in so doing accepted the crown that people had proferred too soon. He had become, at last, a total jazz musician, the man that his followers would have had us believe he was in 1947 and then again in 1949. Still only twenty-nine, he now demonstrated none of his earlier inhibitions. He was not floating pilot balloons but launching into solos that had shape, purpose and the almost impossible synthesis of tension and relaxation.

More important, there was a guile, intellect and natural, melodic gift evident in his solos. Graham Boatfield observed (*Jazz Journal* January '59) that he 'gave the impression of being able to improvise endlessly and *well* – for hours if necessary.' Certainly his reconstruction of popular ballads transformed them, replacing the charm of *There Is No Greater Love, It Never Entered My Mind, Surrey With The Fringe On Top* and *When I Fall In Love* with a natural melancholy and, above all, a profundity that made sense of Art Blakey's classification 'today's classical music'.

Superficially, the most distinguishing feature of his work of the period was that he had taken to using the harmon mute. This gave his tone a smoke glass quality and, as Ian Carr (5) astutely pointed out, 'intensified the impact of the solos because the wild feeling seemed bottled-in'.

Davis had changed the rules. The great jazz soloists of almost any era, and that includes the free experimental period, observed the climactic element in solo building. A solo should be paced from its take-off point through its central re-examination section and then finally should reach an emotional climax or at least a powerful resolution.

Davis's solos were like the sea plane that never takes off. They clipped the wave tops, rode buoyantly over the harmonic water mass but only rarely did they take to the sky. It was an attitude compatible with his personality. It was as if he was saying that his audiences should accept his mode of improvisation as it stood; he was not giving out travel brochures and if the listener required the stratosphere they should travel on another air-line.

This was his strength, even before the free formers; his music was saying 'judge every stage of a solo on its own merits'. Most instrumentalists adopt this policy with the blues; Davis saw no reason to adjust it, whatever the material. In fact, the medium blues was often one of his most fertile production areas; he avoided the clichés that the form can offer, sat on the Garland superstructure and filled out his allotted space with a sense of grieving aggression.

He still avoided the extremes of the range but began to essay up tempo items with far greater confidence. The ghosts of technically-equipped giants like Dizzy Gillespie and Fats Navarro were no longer on his shoulder and the odd note malformation did not deter him. The creative process was more important than empty niceties and Davis was setting standards that marked him out as one of the finest of all jazz improvisers. He was, nevertheless, still part of the quintet and it would be both pointless and incorrect to see his own contribution as a thing apart.

One of the important factors that fostered this spirit of mutual co-operation was the manner in which the bulk of the quintet's recordings were made. Not for Davis the protracted multi-session, with endless retakes and splicings. The main body of the quintet's finest work was made for the Prestige label in two days, one in May and the other in October 1956. It was as if the band reported to the studio on each occasion and placed a major part of its current repertoire on historical file.

Only in the sense that the music was timeless can one accept its historical position. In reality, it was vibrant jazz before anything else, not only at the vanguard of musical development but with a spontaneity that made its creation sound almost casual. More significantly, it embraced a range of expression that made it impossible to classify in terms of a Miles Davis 1956 style. There were no formulas for ballads, no set tempos for blues nor was there any order of solo sequence. Each selection was taken on its own merits. Davis played through his harmon mute, or open as the case demanded but, more significantly, he sounded more relaxed than ever before.

This attitude permeated the whole group and never more noticeably than in the case of John Coltrane. His earliest recordings with Davis, from the previous year, had about them a tension that arrested his melodic as well as rhythmic flow. There had been times when the tenor saxophonist had seemed determined to get his elaborate ideas across, whatever the time available within each chorus. It was an act of cramming that robbed his solos of both grace and inner balance and it was remarkable how one year in the constant musical proximity of Miles Davis matured him.

He said to Valerie Wilmer (*Jazz Journal* – December 1962) that 'I used to want to play tenor the way he (Davis) played trumpet, when I used to listen to his records. But when I joined him I realized I could never play like that, and I think that's what made me go the opposite way'. The detail and verbosity of his playing was certainly a contrast to the Davis trumpet delivery but being with Davis concentrated his thinking patterns and slowed his mind to accommodate his torrential delivery. It was as if he had suddenly found room to say all he needed.

Despite this growing compatibility, there were other problems. Davis could not always be relied upon to keep his bookings and critic Bill Cole (6) is just one of many who reports having turned up to hear the quintet only to be told that Davis had cancelled at short notice. The excuses varied but Davis's circumstances had changed. Drug addiction had broken his marriage but now he was cured. He was again taking pride in his appearance and it is more than likely that his later reputation as an exceptionally sharp dresser began at this time. He was certainly taking interest in pretty girls and had begun to live the life expected of a handsome *bon vivant*. It was not a situation conducive to establishing confidence in the minds of either his followers or his prospective employers.

More serious, from a musical point of view, was an event that occurred in the November of 1956, when Davis and Coltrane abruptly parted company. Shortly before this, Thelonious Monk is reputed to have seen 'Miles slap Trane in the face and then punch him in the stomach' (4) during a backstage altercation at the Bohemia. Whatever the actual details of their difference, the outcome was that the tenor saxophonist joined the Monk group on a permanent basis.

In the ensuing year Davis toured Europe and reunited with arranger Gil Evans for a musical association of tremendous importance. This will be discussed later but, back in New York, Davis used his old colleague Sonny Rollins and, toward the end of 1957, alto saxophonist Julian "Cannonball" Adderly for combo engagements.

For Davis, however, it was not a wholly satisfactory arrangement and, in November 1957, he simply called his former tenor man and arranged for his return to the group. Adderley remained, the quintet became a sextet, and Davis again had the tools to build the next stage of his career. At last, his popularity in Europe was being matched in his homeland, he was winning polls, and was in demand as an artist. His fame was also spreading on non musical fronts and, because of his sartorical trend setting, his 'hip' attitudes and his success with ladies, he was marked out as a special man. Personally, he seemed to be unimpressed by this type of attention, but his status as a cult figure was ratified in 1958, when Time magazine printed an article on him.

Davis remained more concerned with his music, and his six-piece band was on the brink of producing some of the most theoretically important and musically beautiful records in the history of jazz. In many ways, the climate was just right. In California, Ornette Coleman was making his first revolutionary, free form records and there was a mood of discovery in the jazz world. Davis had, for some time, sought to extend the freedom available to his sidemen and to himself. He moved away from the harmonic sequence, the super-structure of the traditional bebop improvisation, and began to use scales as a lead-off point for his inventive processes. The key centre remained constant but, by the permutation of related, scalar patterns, he achieved a freedom that suited his own melodic requirements and presented his sidemen with acceptable licence.

Davis took that latitude to the ultimate on the sextet's first recording. He personally laid out on one title and, on another, made no attempt to feature himself. Pianist Red Garland did not play at all on *Sid's Ahead* and Davis shunned the harmon mute throughout. *Milestones*, the album's title track, was the really important one. It was one of his first modal pieces and it demonstrated not only his new approach but, also, the extent of his detachment from Charlie Parker and the music of the era. It was built on only two scales and Ian Carr (5) perceptively observed that "harmony had become decorative rather than functional".

The impromptu element remained important and one had only to listen to the way in which Davis picked up on an Adderley phrase at the start of his *Milestones* solo to appreciate the fact. No solo had a prepared introduction and there was an audacity about all six musicians that made mutual inspiration a modus operandi.

Good as the 'Milestones' album had been, the sextet's next was magnificent. With either Bill Evans or Wynton Kelly in place of Garland and with Jimmy Cobb in the drum chair, the group recorded 'Kind Of Blue' over two recording dates in March and April 1959. The musicians involved had never before played any of the selections and Bill Evans said of the session 'Miles conceived these settings only hours before the recording date, and arrived with sketches which indicated to the group what was to be played. Therefore you will hear something close to true spontaneity in these performances.'

How true this was. In fact, Evans actually finalized all of the arrangements on the date and, although composer honours were credited to the leader, it was the pianist who claimed to have originally written *Blue In Green* and *Flamenco Sketches*. Not that this really mattered, because this was a record to put alongside the likes of Louis Armstrong's Okehs, the Charlie Parker Savoy/Dials and the Ornette Coleman Altantics. It was one of jazz's finest moments.

Teo Macero, himself a musician as well as a writer of atonal classical works, was the producer. He was very much in sympathy with the project and exerted the minimum of interference. The music was modal throughout, with each player taking advantage of the freedom from chordal restrictions and spinning out his own story. Davis and Coltrane brought an inexorable logic to compositions that had been built on scales, and were not melodic hothouse plants that might have needed to be artificially nurtured. There was a formal logic about their performances that concentrated the listener's attention but, more importantly, there was unashamed beauty.

Some observers might regard it as invidious to pick out individual performances but, seen from the standpoint of Miles Davis, it was a triumph. *Blue In Green* offered one of his most poignant solos on record, while on *Freddie Freeloader* he brought a searing yet terse reality to the basic twelve-bar form. Perhaps the spirit of the whole session was most graphically captured on *So What* where the trumpeter, despite one fleeting technical mishap, sets the mood for his colleagues with a truly magnificent solo. Not suprisingly it was the title chosen to be featured in the CBS film made by the sextet, minus an ailing Adderley, in the April, between the two sessions.

Artistic Sketches

To get these magnificent performances in true perspective it is important to back track to 1957. At that time there had been little contact between Davis and his arranging colleague on the Capitol dates, Gil Evans. The Canadian had been freelancing in comparative obscurity in New York and, although he had produced some octet charts for Charlie Parker and a tentet for Teddy Charles, he was mainly occupied arranging for quality singers like Peggy Lee.

Teaming with Davis changed this state of affairs and also his status in the jazz world. The man who had built *Boplicity*, was now ready to extend his musical estate, and in Davis he had an internationally famous figure to ensure that his work was again heard worldwide. In the event their 'first' recording 'Miles Ahead', spread over four dates in May 1957, was a triumph. Evans used a nineteen piece orchestra and Davis's flugelhorn was the only solo voice. In many ways it was a logical extension of the Capitol ideal. There was no orthodox reed section and the absence of tenor saxophones was compensated for by the use of french horns in the tenor range. As before, the lower register of the band held special attractions for Evans but there was no loss of balance. In fact, English critic Max Harrison was at length to point out that 'In any given chord, careful consideration is given to the best instrument to play each constituent note. The weight of that instrument is most sensitively calculated in relation both to the others used and to the particular effect the chord is meant to have'. The perceptive Harrison had summed up a change of musical attitudes that was to have, in the long term, an effect on Davis's music.

Evans's attention to detail on these sessions was phenomenal; the members of the band were seated to ensure that the ensemble texture was just as he 'heard' it in his head and the personnel was selected with meticulous care. He drew the parent compositions from widely disparate sources but, in the event, transformed them into pure Evans. Davis used flugelhorn although, on the CBS film that remade *The Duke, New Rhumba* and *Blues For Pablo* with a different line up, he took certain parts on trumpet.

The title track was a superb blues arrangement and Davis's solo was a masterpiece of understatement. Throughout the few sessons he played with similarly controlled authority and the critics did not have to rely on hindsight to acclaim it as a brilliant achievement for both men. Stanley Dance, previously a grudging admirer of Davis, was almost alone when he observed (*Jazz Journal,* '58), 'Although great skill has gone into the writing and the performance, the record is fundamentally a pretentious and well glossed sample of the old inferiority complex'.

On the surface, this could be taken as prejudice from a notorious reactionary. It is, nevertheless, worth examination in terms of a total appreciation of Miles Davis and his relationship with Evans. As with subsequent ventures, the arranger had placed backgrounds that nurtured his immense talent and had protected him from his own minor frailties. He had chosen the material used astutely and, more vitally, had achieved total success by his own standards. The total package, however, had strayed some distance from the jazz ideal and without the solo inspiration of Davis and without the heart beat of men like Paul Chambers, Art Taylor, Philly Joe Jones and Elvin Jones, the music of the Evans/Davis collaboration could almost qualify as the 'glossed sample' of Dance's jibe. What saves it, is that Evans had a feeling for the jazz phraseology of the fifties and his brass voicings, in particular, owed much to the phrase shapes of his featured soloist. He did not aspire to the inherent jazz pulse of the Count Basie Orchestra but he came as near to a formal realisation of the same principles as a man with his musical principles could reasonably be expected to get.

For his part, Davis was delighted with the outcome. He realised that the gulf between their musical heritages had been bridged, that his own smouldering, latent volcano had been successfully synthesized with the soft breezes of Evans's musical plains.

It was an achievement of some magnitude yet, in 1958, the two men introduced a third element, one that enlarged the challenge by adding the constriction of using only the compositions of one writer, and from one musical show! The one chosen was *Porgy and Bess*, the composer was George Gershwin and again the project was spread over four sessions.

In some ways, the outcome could be seen as lending rather more credibility to Dance's attitude than had 'Miles Ahead'. It was certainly a triumph but, since it concentrated on one show, it took its form from Evans's personal conception of that work. The piece had originally been written as an opera and Davis had been required to usurp the singer's role. With Evans's aid he had done so with great sensitivity and had produced a performance of timeless beauty.

In pure jazz terms, however, one point must be conceded. Had Davis chosen to work with another arranger, the final product would have been somewhat diminished. Had Evans chosen another soloist, there would have been no great performance to discuss. Thankfully, they did make it and *Porgy and Bess* can be appreciated as a logical advance on their 1957 venture. It had the triumph of *Summertime*, where Evans and Davis became as one. It had *Prayer (Oh Doctor Jesus)*, a slowed down baptist meeting that predated Charles Mingus's more violent *Wednesday Night Prayer Meeting*. Only the calls of the strawberry woman, juxtaposed with the song *Fisherman*, defeated the two principals. On stage, Helen Dowdy had transformed the 'calls' into a slice of blues history and somehow rendered it beyond translation into instrumental terms. It was, perhaps, their only minor inefficacy and *Porgy and Bess* became another landmark in Davis's career.

If there was one of the Davis/Evans collaborations that returned thoughts to Stanley Dance it was 'Sketches of Spain'. It certainly could be seen as the jazzman's reaction to the 'old inferiority complex', the need to compete with classical music and to gain approval by the standards of the conservatoire. The 'Sketches' answered the challenge completely, all the elements came together and the result was a genuine work of art as well as an undisputed jazz performance.

Made in 1959 and the early part of 1960, it found Davis in inspired form reflecting the events of the previous year and most especially 'Kind of Blue'. It came about, as Nat Hentoff tells (in his liner notes), 'because when Miles was on the West Coast early in 1959, a friend had played him a recording of *Concierto de Aranjuez* for guitar and orchestra by the contemporary Spanish composer, Joaquin Rodrigo'.

Hentoff goes on to tell how Davis had said, 'I couldn't get it out of my mind. Then when Gil and I decided to do this album, I played him the record and he liked it. As we usually do, we planned the programme first by ourselves for about two months. I work out something; he takes it home and works on it some more; and then we figure out how we're going to do it. He can read my mind and I can read his'. Classical composer Hal Overton was present on one of the three sessions and is reputed to have described the arrangements as 'the toughest notation' he had seen on a jazz date. Producer Teo Macero thought the writing 'almost Gregorian', yet there is a spontaneity about Davis's playing that belies the circumstances of the recording. He stumbles a little on *Saeta* but elsewhere plays with a mixture of assurance and creativity.

He felt that Evans had made the orchestra sound like 'one big guitar' but this underestimated the extent to which Davis himself entered into the Spanish mood of the work. There are even moments in *Aranjuez* where the phraseology of American jazz takes second place to the fanfare delivery of the bull ring. What Davis did was totally to immerse himself in the dramatic form pecular to the Iberian peninsula. The slow tempos were a severe test of his rhythmic and instrumental powers, and the transfer to ethnic motives examined his ability to transmit his emotional involvement into apparently alien areas. Both challenges were answered impressively, as were traces of Andalusian, Catalonian and Basque folk music threaded one suspects, unconsciously through the St. Louis jazz ethos.

It was obvious that the Davis/Evans orchestra could hardly embark on extensive promotional tours, even if they had so desired. The cost would have been prohibitive but, more significantly, many of the most favoured sidemen had commitments that would have prevented them touring extensively. They did, however, appear in concert on both the east and west coasts. The shows were something of a package, with a section reserved for the quintet, and with Evans continually writing new material.

It was an arrangement that worked, on and off, through the

sixties. Some concerts were recorded and issued, at least in parts, on records, while others, including a near complete remake of 'Sketches' in 1961, were recorded and held in the Columbia vaults. It remained a productive partnership for the two men. Evans treated each changing, musical situation with sympathy and, although it meant restricting his natural musical oratory, Davis accepted the disciplines that were necessary to produce a homogeneous final product.

There was no doubting the quality of subsequent works, but it was *Miles Ahead, Porgy* and *Sketches* that were the pinnacles of this unique association. In retrospect, however, they can be seen as projects that were divorced from the evolutionary jazz mainstream. They were in a position somewhat akin to the music of Duke Ellington. Jazz would have still progressed in the same ineluctable way had neither Ellington nor Evans brought their genius to the cause. Instrumentalists have always been the evolutionary giants and Davis was no stranger to the jazz vanguard. In endless discussions, Davis had been happy to draw off Evans's reservoir of knowledge but it was his quintet and sextet that had ushered jazz into its next theatre of artistic growth.

Marking Time

The artistic, aesthetic and financial success of the Davis/Evans partnership was very welcome, but Davis's career continued to flourish on all fronts. He had begun to enjoy a following of almost 'pop-star' proportions, he was driving a Ferrari, had bought property and was reported by Leonard Feather in *Melody Maker* (17 September 1960) to be asking almost $4000 for an engagement. He had begun to wear 'designer' clothes and had found himself the subject of a fashion article in a leading magazine.

His fame was now such that to some extent it turned to notoriety. His determination to put music first meant that he made few concessions to his audience in the way of visual presentation. It was an aspect of his art that, if anything, endeared him to his supporters and to the critics whose only concern was with his music. Opponents, on the other hand, found his lack of announcements disquieting. They were even more disturbed by his habit of turning his back on the audience. They overlooked the fact that he had always tended to behave like this and the game of Miles Davis baiting began.

Davis ignored them, at least in public, but in the fall of 1959 he did have to face a more tangible manifestation of prejudice. He was working at New York's Birdland club and during an interval was taking a breath of fresh air outside. Despite his assurance that he was actually playing at the club, a police patrolman insisted that he 'move on'. The events of the next few moments are not clear but Davis was beaten about the head with a night stick and ended up in prison. Eye witnesses have spoken of unprovoked police brutality but the cruelest outcome was that the innocent trumpeter temporarily lost his cabaret card – his passport to work in New York!

Davis was completely exonerated in court and his card returned, but it was an unsavoury incident and a reminder that, despite his standing in music, he was still vulnerable to the 'red neck' extremist.

Early in the next year he had to face a different but no less disturbing development. His star sideman John Coltrane had continued to develop artistically and had built up a personal following to rival his leader. The time was ripe for him to go out on his own and, after a European tour in 1960, he left the band never to return.

It would be wrong to ignore the hiatus that this caused, but Davis was in good shape to face the problems. His first choice as a replacement was Sonny Stitt, a decision that suggested a desire to continue the Parker-Adderley lineage. Here was the most gifted of all the Parker inspired altoists and, as a bonus, he was also an outstanding and inexplicably under-rated tenor man. Davis had admired the fleet coherence of Adderley and had used him as a complementary rather than contrasting adjunct to his own playing. Stitt was tailor made to do the same job and, indeed, the partnership worked rather well. Regrettably, it was short lived and, after a few engagements and a European tour, Davis was forced to look elsewhere.

As compatible as Stitt had been, it was still an arrangement that spoke of temporary expediency rather than a major stylistic 'rethink'. His next choice was similar and it came in the person of Hank Mobley, a fine Georgian tenor saxophonist who could boast experience with Max Roach, Dizzy Gillespie and the Jazz Messengers. At the time, a man with such hard bop credentials seemed an ideal partner for Davis, but it was not a team that wrote much Miles Davis lore.

It was perhaps a fact that Davis rarely related to his horn men. The exceptions were the recently departed Stitt and, of course, Coltrane and Adderley; but with Mobley there was little stylistic interaction. It hardly seemed to matter what the newcomer played, as long as it was coherent in its own right. Davis's music has never essayed much in the way of counterpoint and, since he was playing well himself, he required only that Mobley do likewise. Solos were juxtaposed like bricks in a wall, they stood firmly beside each other but there was no molecular overlap, no lead from one to the other. This was not a situation that served Mobley well; titles such as *Oleo*, with Davis taking chances at speed and surprising at every turn, tended to make Mobley sound somewhat bland by comparison. His gently contoured phrases were hardly designed to shock and his considerable creative flair was masked by his smoothness of line and easy execution.

It could well be that the problem of note placement, an occasional affliction in his earlier work, had made him wary of rhythmic extravagances. The oblique look that Davis might take at a melody line came over as a gauntlet thrown down, and Mobley was sometimes a trifle cautious about picking it up. To face the challenge, he built his solos slowly, nurtured his better ideas with care and let them spread logically. The outcome was better than the superficial observer might imagine.

The only conflict that arose was in the fact that Mobley, himself something of a revolutionary voice in the late fifties, had not pushed his style through the mangle of the free revolution. Davis, in contrast, had been a proxy partner in that phase of the music. More importantly, he had listened to its often wilder elements. His own personality, however, had made it impossible for him to embrace its folkish or, as he complained, amateurish aspects. The intuitive skills of the free formers jarred and, although he admired Ornette Coleman for avoiding clichés, he was suspicious of many of his stylistic partners.

Certainly as an overall concept, the bluesy music of the Texan was unacceptable to him. In Davis's book, its richness of melody was hardly enough to compensate for its harmonic naivity and, in rejecting it on those terms, he perhaps did less than justice to some of jazz's true innovators. Where he did pay credit was unconsciously, and then from within his own music. There were times in this period when the stylistic nod toward Coleman's trumpeter Don Cherry was made. Stanley Crouch, in his sleeve note for 'Live At The Plugged Nickel', cites *All Blues* as an example of Davis 'examining some of Cherry's ideas'. This was, of course, a 1965 recording but there was plenty of evidence before that.

This goes some distance toward explaining why the presence of Mobley was acceptable, rather than inspiring. In fact, it would seem that Davis was not altogether committed to facing a new challenge of quite the Coltrane magnitude in the early sixties. Among the alternatives were Jimmy Heath and, far more surprisingly, Eric Dolphy.

This enigmatic alto saxophonist, flautist and bass clarinettist had often been associated with the Coleman axis of the free movement although, in reality, he had very little to do with it. For Davis to consider him as a possibility for the group was an unexpected step, especially as, in a later (1964) *Down Beat* Blindfold test, he identified Dolphy because 'nobody else could sound that bad'.

Dolphy's position in jazz history has always been vague. He had been likened to Coleman by some observers but his style, for all its brilliantly conceived irregularity, was based on constant harmonic progressions. In contrast to Coleman, there was a distinct element of romanticism in his style, he made modest use of rococo decoration and this gave his line a grace that reminded us of the rhapsodic saxophonists of the forties.

He would have perhaps been the challenge that Davis needed. He would certainly have not introduced the free melodic association of Coleman, but what he could have offered was a third alternative to the routes taken by the Texan and by Davis's own unique sextet. In the final reckoning, he failed to join the band and Davis continued his search.

In 1963, Mobley was replaced by George Coleman, a twenty-eight year old tenor saxophonist from Memphis, Tennessee. Despite his background, his playing at the time showed little trace of the heavy southern states musical dialect. If anything, there was something of Stan Getz in his sound and in the way he built his solos.

This in itself gradually caused a minor dichotomy within the group. It was unconsciously encouraged by further changes in the band made shortly after the arrival of Coleman, when Davis brought in Herbie Hancock and Tony Williams. Pianist Hancock had become something of a house pianist for the thriving Blue Note record company and was a stylist who brought grace, facility and inventive-ness to his duties there. If anything, Davis's choice was a continuation of the tradition begun with Red Garland and Wynton Kelly. Like them, Hancock could match flowing 'tune playing' with strong chordal work and, if required, could lay out when the leader sought greater harmonic freedom.

Tony Williams was a Bostonian drum prodigy who had worked with Sam Rivers. He was fast and loud and, in spite of his youth, a man with strong personal convictions about the drum's role in the modern combo. The far reaching effect of his arrival will be discussed later but in 1963 he represented for Davis another extrovert drummer to be tamed.

In the short term it was an effect made slightly more obvious by George Coleman. The tenor saxophonist struck up an immediate musical affinity with Hancock and it was almost as if, together, they felt something of the lyricism of the Teddy Wilson and Lester Young era. The backbone of hard bop was still there but their musical dialogue enjoyed its own moments of rhetoric.

The effect within the quintet was perhaps to accentuate the relationship between the leader and Williams, his new young drummer. Earlier in the band's life Davis had thought that the new rhythm section had been more uninhibited behind Coleman. The band's work of the time does not support this theory but it may well explain why Davis sought an affinity with Williams rather than his colleagues. Certainly, their rapport grew rapidly and, while there was no question of a split in the total sense, there did seem to be an occasional lack of unity within the group.

If there was a small element of turmoil it was not a new phenomenon. Davis has always had the ability to take on an unruly and loud rhythm team and shape it in his own image. No loss of virility ever occurred and there was never a hint of rhythmic castration. As if to ensure this, it was the drummer, rather than the bassist, who remained at the centre of Davis's rhythm sections. It was a tradition that had reached its full potential with Philly Joe Jones but it also had special meaning for Williams.

As always, the turmoil was short lived and, with the brilliant Ron Carter now the permanent bassist, the band undertook a far eastern tour in 1964. By this time Coleman had become dissatisfied with various aspects of his relationship with his leader and had left. At his new drummer's suggestion, Davis replaced him with Sam Rivers and the band flew out with a saxophonist who had but the sketchiest knowledge of the quintet's 'book'.

It was also an unlikely choice in other ways, because it brought to the unit a man who had listened constructively to, and had great respect for, Ornette Coleman and Cecil Taylor. His admiration for the other wing of the vanguard did not direct his playing too far outside the parameters set by Davis, however, and one could be tempted to imagine Rivers' route being akin to that which Dolphy might have taken.

For his part, he was never entirely happy and he told Michael Ullman (7) that he had just declined a chance to join Art Blakey because he was 'already past bebop'. He had actually been working with blues giant T-Bone Walker when asked to join Davis and the change to the rarified atmosphere of the trumpeter's quintet must have been something of a shock. Davis was certainly a daunting figure and, at the time, Rivers said 'I believe that some musicians who went through Miles' bands were just as impressed with his life style as they were with his music'.

Strangely enough, Rivers was not impressed and he left the group to embark on a far more precarious career, one that later led him to the position of club owner and something of an avant garde guru to the young jazzmen who created their own clubs in the attics of New York warehouses. His own Studio Rivbea was one such club and played an important part in the 'loft movement' of the seventies. Nevertheless, Rivers' brief stay with Davis was not musically uneventful.

Faced by his magnificent work in the immediately preceeding years, it was inevitable that certain observers would have reservations about the Miles Davis of the early sixties. They were not worried by his own playing, nor were they perturbed by his constant changes of playing companions. They held, and not without some justification, that his material had stagnated, that he returned continually to favourite tunes, speeding them up for stimulation, but rarely equalling his earlier versions of them.

Ironically, Rivers showed what could be done with oft recorded items like *So What* and *Walkin'* even if they were taken at seemingly unsuitable up tempi. He made no attempt at full frontal attack, his timing was more oblique, he feinted and sidestepped, occasionally grumbled his way over bar divisions yet always presented his argument persuasively. Davis, for all his creative impetus, was rhythmically more orthodox by comparison, a point that would certainly not have escaped his own notice. He had always been his own sternest critic and he was soon to show himself prepared for yet another step forward.

Extrasensory Perception

If, in retrospect, the years of the early sixties were taken as something of a marking time period in the Davis saga, they were certainly not an aesthetic desert. They actually set the stage for the musical expansion that occured in the middle of the decade, even if they will never be seen as being as revolutionary as the 1949 Capitols or as iconoclastic as 'Kind Of Blue'. Rather, they were changes by observable stages.

The real change came with the arrival of Wayne Shorter. He had already been on one recording date with Miles in 1962 but, in 1964, he joined on a permanent basis. His pedigree was impeccable. He had been one of Art Blakey's most illustrious Messengers and, during nearly four years in the band, had established himself as a stalwart and creative saxophonist. He also emerged as a composer of no mean ability, a good tactical arranger and, on stage, a firm 'straw boss'.

His overriding influence was Coltrane, and Brian Case likened his playing (8) to 'a savage rip-saw' and compared 'listening to his weirdly asymmetrical lines to being knocked down by a chess player'. Certainly there was the paradox of fierce attack and logical progression, things that Miles was to exploit in the ensuing years as Shorter became co-author of a very vital chapter in the Davis book. His enrolment was the final factor in encouraging Gil Evans to describe (again) the new group as the best band in the world. Such declarations are questionable, but the trumpeter's motives and actions over the next five years are worthy of detailed examination.

51

In previous bands, the interaction between Davis's own overall concept and that of his fellow players or arrangers led only to changes of musical direction. At no time did the influence of any of them deflect the trumpeter from his own *instrumental course*. The visual impression of him ignoring their solo efforts was not far from reality and if there was any evidence of instant influence it came as *they* took minor stylistic transfusions from *him*.

The major changes of musical direction were sometimes radical but, in terms of the practicalities of performance, the playing of sidemen hardly altered Davis's own technique at all. His phrase shapes had remained basically the same, his sense of timing was refined very little and his tone had taken on only a slightly deeper burr. The formation of this group saw a gradual movement away from this state of affairs.

The new quintet was captured on record for the first time while performing at the Berliner Jazztage '64 in the Philharmonic Hall. The rhythm section had been together for four months and that fact was immediately apparent. Davis had made no attempt to shackle his drummer and, although Williams was somewhat under-recorded, there was a power from behind that served both Davis and Shorter alike.

As had been the vogue for some time, the new line-up used known tunes but, almost immediately, there was a change. There was a freshness of discovery about the group that transcended the material used. This was a matter of especial satisfaction to Davis, now working with Shorter, whom he had failed to woo from Blakey some two years earlier. The saxophonist had been reluctant to make the change at that time because in the Messengers he was a leading light. He was encouraged to write and arrange and he could always hear his new works in instant performance.

If he had feared that joining Davis would have deprived him of that advantage, he was wrong. He was given the chance to write straight away and did so to good effect. Tunes such as *E.S.P.* and *Iris* were used in Davis's first studio recording in well over a year, and they proved to be very fine vehicles for the group. Certainly the leader found them inspirational and on *Iris* showed that he was still intent on taking the chance route, thinking as far ahead as necessary and certainly not making long term plans in his improvisational path.

The whole of this January 1965 session was a success and it

provided the first recorded evidence of Davis's retreat from fixed chorus lengths. His entire rhythmic and melodic style had 'loosened up' and Ian Carr (5) provided a brilliant insight when he saw that 'the essence of this way of playing is as follows: a melodic fragment sets up the theme of the performance; a pulse (usually 4/4 or 3/4), a tempo, and a series of phrases played against that pulse. The improvisations are explorations of these factors posited by the theme, and so the soloist tends to refer back to thematic fragments.'

How near it had come to Ornette Coleman and the free association of his melodic snippets! In fairness, modern recording techniques did offer insurance against the hazards of such an instantaneous policy and, on *Iris*, the use of a tape splice suggests strategic editing. There were, however, live recordings to attest to Davis's continuing extempore attitudes. As with the Jazztage '64 session, these dates still used established material and thereby invited comparisons with previous versions of the same tune.

Typical were the two days at the Plugged Nickel in Chicago when the quintet was recorded near to the height of its powers. Every title was a well used Davis favourite but the treatment was unequivocally adventurous. There was, however, one incident on the date that showed an unexpected side to the Davis mentality. The opening of *Round Midnight* was chaotic. At first it seemed like a series of false starts and there were sympathetic reactions from the audience. Bad note production was a feature of the trumpeter's own theme statement and an exaggerated 'blue' note lent a sour quality to the phrase that included it. The rhythm section was lost in the confusion and it was not until Shorter took over the solo spot that there was any positive direction.

Such events are hardly unknown in a music as spontaneous as jazz, and Davis always seemed on the point of drawing in the reins and getting the band organised. Suprisingly he did not and, in fact, embarked on a deliberate (?) course of trumpet chicanery.

On other occasions he had been highly critical of the 'amateurish' techniques exhibited by certain of the 'new wave' musicians. He had refused to accept, as chromatic licence, their excesses of note bending and had put coherent expression as a very high priority in his art of music making. Parody was not one of his aesthetic tools and, if a tune deserved such treatment, it had no place in his repertoire.

Round Midnight would certainly not have invited derisory treatment and Davis had a good record of working with Thelonious Monk compositions. There was also the point that, had he so chosen, Davis could have refused to allow this title to be issued on record. His days of skuffling were over, he was now an international figure, very much in control of his own artistic destiny. Whether it was to slight the charlatans of the *avant garde's* second phase or to remind his own sycophants of the realities of the creative process, he allowed the item to be issued.

Unfortunately, the next twelve month period, between the *ESP* studio date and the Plugged Nickel engagement, was an unhappy one for Davis. An extremely painful hip became unbearable and an operation was essential. He was hospitalized for four months and even after release was reduced to using crutches for some time. In fact, he actually left hospital before the recommended time and was repaid for his exuberance with a heavy fall and a broken leg. This inevitably affected his playing opportunities and finally, eighteen months were to elapse between *ESP*, his first studio date with the group, and the second, *Miles Smiles*.

The irony of this title was obvious but there were some compensations. Davis had been able to re-assemble his group without loss and to get back to the kind of unity that they had previously displayed. Both horn players were still reacting to the rhythmic challenge thrown down by the Williams inspired rhythm team, but they were doing so by making contact only when it suited them. Spaces were left deliberately and an almost detached air prevailed.

Shorter in particular mellowed at this time. The abrasive, almost irrascible, saxophone sound assumed a more brotherly fervour. There was no diminution of power but the more refined auditory sensations seemed to invite the listener to join him rather than, as before, demanding that they should. His compositions remained a major factor and it was hardly surprising that a truly memorable theme like *Footprints* should produce one of the timeless Davis performances from this now totally integrated unit.

In view of later developments it would be dangerous to underplay the rhythmic changes that had taken place. Hancock was essentially a fleet and intricate soloist in the Davis tradition, but there were times when he sat out of the proceedings or, more significantly, became part of a two or three man vamp behind the horns. With drummer Williams a permanent power source it was still possible for his piano to take a Bill Evans-like route and he still did this very impressively.

The rhythmic vamps, however, did become more significant and, for the first time, there must be a suggestion that Davis was taking audiences into his confidence. In certain moody performances, the quintet would build up a simple ostinato using sometimes as few as three notes. This repeated phrase would be spread over the opening choruses until the listener's ear became unconsciously aware of it. With its removal, he was left to continue the phase as a mental process. In fact, the listener became part of the performance himself.

There were other departures from the Davis tradition at the time, even to the extent of group performances that did not feature a single Davis solo. *Nefertiti* showed how Davis could reiterate and colour a good theme statement for nearly eight minutes without a trace of boredom. Such a performance took us nearest to the heart of the man; no effort was made to play for effect and the listener could almost sense the trumpeter's desire to communicate at a basic level. This did not entail playing down, the theme was merely allowed to breath, and the outcome was unmistakably the work of Davis. His personality was in every note, the timing was uniquely his, and tone was a beacon that led a generation of copyists.

In this quintet, every player got to make solo statements, and only rarely were they organic continuations of the theme. Each was more of a personal exposition, using the Davis dialect and filling its moments in time without responsibility for what might follow. Davis remained the stylistic leader but, listening to the group at the 1967 London Jazz Expo, one was struck by the increasing importance of drummer Williams.

Few people could have guessed, however, that it would be Williams, rather than a horn player, that would become the first instrumentalist to encourage genuine stylist change, not only in Davis's general musical concept but also in his personal style.

Philly Joe Jones had never been a mere backroom boy in the rhythm section but his role had been to provide colouration in the ensemble and to give rhythmic impetus to the solo voices. This he had done brilliantly without moving out of the rhythm section. Tony Williams was an entirely different proposition. He started to play a part in the Davis ethic that was musical, spiritual and inspirational.

In musical terms, he had become a powerful voice, on equal footing with the horns but, more significantly he had introduced an intensity that spoke of the then avant garde movement in a way that Davis and his sidemen had previously avoided. The spiritual aspect was altogether different. In one way it tied in with the trumpeter's general attitude towards free jazz and the other modern forms that rubbed shoulders with his music in the late sixties. Davis was faced with the problem of wishing to develop along lines acceptable to his own standards, while still embracing the new sounds he heard around him. At a club date he invited Archie Shepp to sit in with him then stormed off because the tenor saxophonist hogged the solo limelight, playing jazz with which he had little sympathy.

Davis had reason to be satisfied with the progress his own music had made, yet he was not entirely content. He could not accept the bulk of free jazz because the freedom that was its raison d'être offended his very being. When confronted with the New York Contemporary Five, he told Leonard Feather that he 'didn't understand that jive at all'. He genuinely saw people that enjoyed it as 'gullible' and in the same interview (9) said, 'If something sounds terrible, man, a person should have enough respect for his own mind to say it doesn't sound good. It doesn't to me, and I'm not going to listen to it.'

The rhythmic power of free form jazz is sometimes held in check and this was another minus factor for Davis, one that he publicly denounced. Yet, for all of his rhythmic élan, the young Williams had showed that he too could grasp the implictions of a more static approach and a title like *Nefertiti* was an object lesson in vital drumming at slow tempo.

The London Odeon cinema concerts of 1967 had given perhaps more idea of the quintet's musical direction than had contemporary records. Surprisingly he found himself teamed on a bill with Archie Shepp and had taken the unexpected course of surrendering the 'top of the bill' last set to his junior. The audience, at least for the second performance seemed to be equally divided between the supporters of both teams and it would be wrong to deny the feeling of rivalry that seemed to permeate the hall.

On the night, both bands played continuous performances and

the 'walk-out' during Shepp's final set has been somewhat exaggerated. The significant fact was that Davis made no attempt to offer a Plugged Nickel-type show. His immaculately attired group played a continuous 'shirt sleeves' set lasting just over an hour. Familiar motives were woven into its fabric, solo sequences button holed throughout, and the whole organic music mass was offered for the audience to accept or reject in its entirety.

The music's rhythmic aspect was even more positive. Williams and Carter set up a constant barrage of cross rhythms, shifting beneath the surface of the music and denying Shorter and Davis a soft option. As a result, the horns never relaxed and one sensed that this was a conscious policy, a deliberate strategem to build excitement in the face of the challenge to come. Davis did not use his mute all evening and certainly seemed to relish the faster passages more than his crowd-pleasing harmon dream sequences. It was a tense Davis playing the tense jazz to which he was now totally committed.

Double Image

John Coltrane had died on 17 July 1967 and this re-instated Miles Davis as the unofficial leader of the *avant garde's* 'right wing'. He was, however, becoming increasingly wary of jazz as a museum piece and was worried that, like the Coleman branch of contemporary jazz, his own had a largely white audience. Rock music was on a world-wide high and jazz was experiencing one of its periods of comparative rejection.

Seen in this light, the events that took place from the end of 1968 and for the next seven years, can be put into perspective. Davis rightly felt that he would gain greater acceptance with his 'own people' by meeting them on common ground. He had actually become friendly with rock star Jimi Hendrix and was enough of an opportunist to realise that, if he was to remain in the public limelight, he had to move towards a different audience and present his music within a package they would understand.

This apparent prostitution was, of course, nothing of the kind and almost by accident it became Davis's passport to a new and vital musical territory. The importance of Williams's contribution was now more obvious and it became increasingly clear that his drumming when first joining the band had been tailored to follow in the Davis quintet tradition. As he gained his head, more was heard of Williams the young man conversant with the intelligent end of popular music. It would be wrong, however, to oversimplify the synthesis that took place. It was not a naive coming together of the leader's linear solo conception and the vertical figures of rock.

Williams was not a rock drummer and he used the more blatant aspects of rock timing merely as a tool, one that opened the door to the type of loose gait that he required.

Herbie Hancock grew increasingly close to Davis at this time. He had also become involved in the soul end of the jazz world and had written his rhythm and blues hit *Watermelon Man*. He became a further voice for rock within the band and when the 'Miles In The Sky' album was made in the summer of 1968, the band had gone electric, at least to the extent that an electric piano, bass and guitar had been used.

Hancock, himself, was initially uncomfortable with the instrument and tended to play it as he would its acoustic brother. The more positive move toward a rock/jazz fusion came, in these early experiments, from Carter's fender bass. As a title like *Stuff* showed, he adopted a more basic stance, stripped his style of its previous ornamentation and became a chaste purveyor of the band's new heart beat.

What made it especially significant was that the return to a simple beat was in direct contrast to the methods employed by the majority of new wave players. They had increasingly placed the responsibility for hearing the beat in the ears of their listeners, rather as Davis had done by the removal of his insistent vamp. Now he had returned to a policy of laying it down for them.

During this time the quintet did not actually introduce much of its rock influenced material into live performances but, towards the end of 1968, English bassist Dave Holland and pianist Chick Corea replaced Carter and Hancock. Corea certainly had a better grasp of Davis's changed requirements and when, early in 1969, Williams finally left the group the transition toward the new order had been rather untidily completed.

Davis was now totally committed to music with a strong and positive pulse and the real breakthrough using contemporary rock rhythms came, early in 1969, with the recording of In A Silent Way. Although he was to leave the band that year, Shorter still had an important part to play although, at short notice, Davis brought in English guitarist John McLaughlin and keyboards specialist Joe Zawinul. With Hancock also recalled for the session, the band boasted three pianists, a strange action for a leader who had often invited his pianists to 'lay out'.

Even more surprising was the fact that Davis laid himself open to the whims of the studio sound mixer for the first time. The last theme statement on *Silent Way* was actually a repeat of the first one, spliced in, and his *Shhh/Peaceful* solo was produced twice to extend the side of the record to an acceptable playing time.

Jazz, by its very nature, is at its best as a live music. Recording tends to re-create artificially the circumstances of the in-person performance but cannot always capture the mood or spirit of the original. To place some of the creative responsibility in the hands of an engineer may not mar the beauty of the final product, but it certainly undervalues it as a true representation of the performer's art. Jazz has never found it necessary to bolster its players with artificial aids and to do so to a musician of Davis's tremendous talent is something of an insult.

In the event, he made a nonsense of such circumstances. The record was a success both commercially and aesthetically and Davis's trumpet work was as moving in this musical environment as it had even been in more orthodox surroundings. The insistent simplicity of some of its backgrounds put his smouldering emotionalism into even starker relief and did nothing to stifle his creativity.

For Davis it was a new stance. Contemporary rock was an input but he remained loyal to the precepts of his jazz heritage and his improvisational method could still be traced to his bebop beginnings. As he had done before, he had taken the aspects of rock that pleased him; he had added an extra dimension to the form and had made it peculiarly his own.

His live performance still made scant reference to rock but his interviews told a different story. There was even an article about him in *Rolling Stone*, the magazine of the rock generation, although this did tend to concentrate on his athletic aspirations and on his interest in the pugilistic art.

Davis was certainly enjoying the attention of his new record buying public. He was fitter than he had been for some time, he was diet conscious and was also playing rather well. It was as if his presence in this 'rock' atmosphere had rekindled his full enthusiasm. His music breathed passion and it declared his total involvement.

This was certainly true of his next venture in the fall of 1969 when, taking an even more expansionistic view, he recorded 'Bitches Brew'. It was a stunning performance although spread over three days but,

60

perhaps for the first time, it showed the effect that the music of Coltrane's later years had had on Davis. Its musical architecture was very different but there was the same incantatory violence, a secular intensity that caught something of the Trane's religious fervour.

Jack DeJohnette was now in the drum chair but there were times when the group boasted what was effectively a nine-man rhythm section. This was ostensibly to give depth to the group, and Davis did seem to deploy his troops sensibly. Nevertheless, tales circulated to the effect that he gave inadequate or muddled instructions to his sidemen. There was probably some truth in this but, it must be remembered, he was himself a newcomer to this wedding of styles and was doing almost as much learning as he was teaching.

Davis seemed to be mainly in control, however, and the rhythm team, for all its numerical strength, had functions that transcended their traditional roles. Ron Brown (*Jazz Journal International*, Sept. 1970) noted that 'they were concerned with more than rhythm. Even during reflective moments there was always some whispering from a drum kit or one of the basses, some brief comments from the bass clarinet, or a faint interjection from a piano'. The horns, apart from Davis, often became part of the rhythm section and the emphasis was given to this department.

Davis ranged freely over this rhythmic swirl and gave his first really extended example of electric trumpet playing. His orthodox horn playing on this 1969 date set the stage, featuring an unusually declamatory and sparse melodic line. Davis, with the 'plugged in' trumpet played 'chords' and put that spare line into its correct context. It was passionate but it was not Davis at his full, creative potential. His status in his own band had taken on the guise of the provider of asides, leaving him to share the main dialogue with his multi-instrumental rhythm team. With other horns doubling on percussion instruments, the rhythmic aspect was occasionally un-wieldly but, as if to acknowledge it, Davis toured with, and made records with, a sextet including two horns as well as his own.

As his sessions with Gil Evans had shown, Davis could become heavily involved with the technicalities of recording. The emphasis on electronics increased his studio commitment, and he showed himself willing to work over pre-recorded backgrounds. These were often his own and *Yesternow*, for instance, made use of a section of *Shhh/Peaceful*.

The strong arm of his rhythm teams was still the drummer and, although Jack DeJohnette was an excellent replacement for Williams, there were always other drummers and sundry percussionists to augment. Billy Cobham deserted his hard bop activities and was briefly one of them but his transition was not an altogether successful one. DeJohnette remained the power source. He was for some time as vital to the music as Davis himself. Much depended on him to ensure that the centreless swirl of the rhythm avoid the worst excesses of the underground pop groups and he filled the role brilliantly.

Superficial listeners and newcomers to Davis's music were beginning to classify the band as a rock unit. This was not a view shared by Davis. He hated any attempt to classify him and told Frederick Murphy in an *Encore* (21 July 1975) interview 'I don't play rock. Rock is a white word and I don't like the word jazz because jazz is a nigger word that white folks dropped on us. We just play black. We play what the day recommends'.

It was a fair comment but Davis's music was jazz based. The situation was further complicated because the band had now begun to divide its activities between making jazz tours and appearing at established pop venues. Fillmore East, a reclaimed cinema, was one such place and the band was recorded there, over four days, in 1970. On all of them, Davis and DeJohnette were superb, even if one could not help but conjecture at the outcome, had the basic pulse been left entirely to DeJohnette's driving drums. More important, Davis made up some ground in regaining the ascendency in his own group, and it was the trumpet that dominated the proceedings.

Concessions were made to the audience, however, and the abstract beginning to the Saturday set and the orgiastic climax to the Thursday night were aimed at a psychedelic awareness. As 'freak-outs' at totally different emotional levels, they were effective but, although brief, they could be construed as an ill omen for the near future.

Certainly not all record issues of the period were as basically consistent and, although *Funky Tonk* showed how well Davis had mastered his electric trumpet and wah wah pedal, the (Live/Evil) collection, taken from assorted sessions, was uneven. What was certain was that Davis had now completely incorporated his basic method into the sound colouration world of rock.

Unfortunately, Davis had not completely formalised his style and, as his dismal concert in London in 1971 showed, he had settled for an uneasy compromise and was employing musical noises as textural entities rather than melodic figures. He was not helped by a weak group and fair minded observers are unlikely to disagree with Pete Gamble (*Jazz Journal International* January 1972) who found the 'rock rhythm section unbelievably muddy' and the leader himself 'definitely uninspired'.

Gamble described how 'he rattled off short bursts of notes, punctuated by lengthy silences with just the rhythm section chugging away'. Regrettably, it was a performance that found a permanent record in the following year when even an improved band failed to inspire its leader to any greater extent when they recorded (On The Corner) in New York.

It was a series of performances that brought into relief the rhythmic poverty of such units. In the band were gifted, rhythmic performers like Herbie Hancock, Chick Corea, John McLaughlin, Mike Henderson, Jack DeJohnette and Billy Hart, as well as a sitar and a tabla player. Their presence, however, was no guarantee of genuine rhythmic complexity and it could be argued that the work of a single drummer like Dannie Richmond or Milford Graves would have offered more in the way of rhythmic displacement, than would this whole collection of rock percussionists.

The main point was that Davis hardly played at all. It was rumoured that he was living the high life on advances from Columbia and was virtually forced to record on a regular basis whether he had anything to say or not. He was quoted in Britain's *Melody Maker* as saying that he was playing for 'the black people' and that was a legend astutely supported by CBS. In their advertising blurb they said 'Take a walk down a city street with Miles Davis and listen to the language of the people on the sidewalk. Listen to music that captures the joy, the pain, the beauty of people who live on "The Block". Listen to one of the most beautiful places in the world'. Too often this meant that audiences were not listening to much Miles Davis.

In a way, Davis' own attitude did not help this situation. He was a man-about-town, he was sought after by beautiful women, wore elegant clothes and drove fast cars. It is an exaggeration to say that he believed his own publicity but he found himself in a situation that literally demanded that he should ignore criticism from whatever source.

Many of his peers were perplexed by his playing and it is of value to quote a devoted admirer like Ian Carr, who pointed out that (5) 'It was (no longer) modal music; it was chromatic improvisation and the basis was a skeletal theme or bass figure'. There could be little complaint with such an observation but Davis was playing less and less.

A 1972 performance at New York's Philharmonic Hall, and another in 1973 at London's Rainbow, gave evidence that Davis was content to be almost a spectator at his own concerts. The often shapeless, rhythmic swirls were still proclaimed as 'ghetto street rhythms' and this was accepted as justification in its own right. The emphasis was on fashion, both musically in the shallow trendiness of the busy, but all too insistent rock backgrounds, and sartorially in the magnificent appearance of this forty-seven year old trumpeter.

Pianist Bob Moses, reported that Davis was booed continually at a German concert and, although this is hardly proof of a valid judgement, it does show that audiences were beginning to think that they had not had their money's worth. In fact, critic David Burnett James gave the most unbiased view when, misled regarding record-ing dates, he saw the 'Big Fun' album as a return to pre- 'On The Corner' standards. His perception was unerring because, what he did not know at the time, was that almost all of that album had come from the period before 'Corner'.

Inevitably the doubters began to speak of the 'emperor's new clothes' while they, themselves, were branded as reactionaries. As always, the truth lay somewhere between these two extremes, although the fact that Davis now had his own travelling hairdresser was not likely to reassure the sceptics. To complicate matters further, record releases were again slowing up, and 'Get Up With It' was an album that presented material spread over an eighteen month period from 1973 to 1974. Apart from *He Loved Him Madly*, the musical content was slight and there was a growing feeling that one of jazz's most major figures was bowing quietly from the scene.

Domestically, the early seventies were not a good time for Davis. He was involved in a couple of law suits and had crossed swords with the Revenue investigators. His voracious appetite for musical discovery was also unsettling him and it was taking him along a path similar to that of the ill-fated Bix Beiderbecke. Davis had 'discovered'

Miles Davis in London, 1967. Photo: David Redfern

above: *The Charlie Parker Quintet at the Three Deuces Club, New York, 1948.*
(l to r) Tommy Potter, Charlie Parker, Max Roach, Miles Davis and Duke
Jordan. Photo: William Gottlieb (David Redfern Photography)

below: *Miles Davis with Gil Evans, 1958.* Photo: Vernon Smith (courtesy
CBS Records).

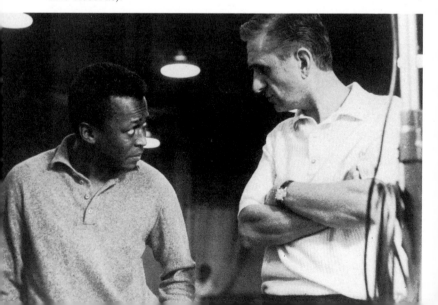

Paul Chambers, John Coltrane and Miles Davis at the Newport Jazz Festival, 1958. Photo: Frank Driggs collection

Miles Davis at the Berlin Jazz Festival, 1964:
above: with Wayne Shorter (tenor sax)
below: with Herbie Hancock (piano) and Tony Williams (drums).
Photos: Jan Persson

Miles Davis in Berlin, 1971 Photo: Jan Persson

above: *Miles Davis at the Berliner Jazztage, 1969* with Dave Holland (bass) and Jack DeJohnette (drums). Chic Corea on keyboards (not visible). Photo: Val Wilmer

below: *Berlin Jazz Festival, 1971.* (l to r) Keith Jarrett (keyboards), Mike Henderson (electric bass), Gary Bartz (alto sax), Leon Chancler (drums), Miles Davis and Don Alias (percussion). Photo: Jan Persson

above: *Miles Davis and John Scofield, at a Concert in Copenhagen in 1984* where Miles received the Leonie Sonning Music Foundation Prize. Photo: Jan Persson

below: *At the Jazz Club Montmartre, Copenhagen, 1984.* (l to r) Bill Evans (soprano and tenor sax), Marcus Miller (bass guitar), Miles Davis and Mike Stern (guitar). Photo: Jan Persson

Miles Davis at the New Orleans Jazz Festival, 1986. Photo: Tim Motion

Karlheinz Stockhausen and, like the legendary Iowan, was having difficulty in reconciling an alien musical form with his own style.

He gave a rather histrionic interview to *Playboy* magazine in which he denigrated his own early triumphs. It was perhaps an act of bravado but it was consistent with the dichotomy that an interest in Stockhausen and his own ghetto aspirations presented. It was also true that, although he had sired a rock/jazz fusion style, bands like Weather Report, with ex-sideman Wayne Shorter, and Herbie Hancock's Headhunters were beginning to out-sell him. Both groups were playing music that was some distance from his but they were doing well in a market created by him and he was justifiably irked.

Unfortunately, Davis's health took a bad turn in 1974; his hip condition deteriorated and he found it necessary to rely on pain killers. Things did not improve in the following year and he had surgery to remove a stomach ulcer as well as to have nodules cut from his throat. His playing became perfunctory and, although he performed at the Newport Festival of 1975, he was playing less.

To make matters worse he also found that he had a hernia and, although this was finally cleared by an operation at the turn of the year, he became something of a recluse. He granted audiences at his home only reluctantly and there were many rumours that he was actually dying.

It Gets Better

Fortunately, the rumours were without grounds and, as jazz moved into the eighties, it was perhaps inevitable that Miles Davis would make a comeback. The reasons for this were various but his life style did cost the kind of money that made even his record royalties seem modest. It is less likely that he missed the limelight, because he had always observed it with intelligent suspicion, but he did miss playing and regarded the return of his trumpet 'chops' as a barometer to gauge his general return to full fitness.

Whatever the reason, New York in the early part of 1981 was buzzing with anticipation. Visitors to the Kool Festival spoke of an earlier session as well as a new record release, and CBS threw a party in Manhattan's Xenon Disco in his honour. Davis himself came, talked to old friends, posed for a barrage of photographers and signed at least one autograph. He looked tired and withdrawn but said he was awaiting his forthcoming concert with enthusiasm.

The concert itself was not an overwhelming triumph. The trumpeter looked and played well but, in a set that lasted almost one and a half hours, had the horn to his lips for little more that ten minutes. Fortunately, when the rumoured record appeared, there were very positive signs of a return to former glories. It contained two unimpressive titles from 1980 and the worst was a soft centred pop melody with a naive eulogy sung by its composer, Randy Hall.

In contrast, the 1981 titles, made before the Xenon party and Kool concert of that year, showed a Davis far more ready for the fray. He played at greater length and, although none of his solos could be described as masterpieces of surprise, they did exhibit a feeling of genuine involvement.

This encouraging trend continued as Davis went on local dates and, toward the end of the year, toured Japan. The band was still not especially strong. Initially saxophonist Bill Evans lacked any real personality, while guitarists Barry Finnerty and Mike Stern were somewhat trapped by rock clichés. The adroit Al Foster was hardly given enough leeway at the drums, but it could be argued that these were contingencies that speeded up their leader's return to grace. The electric band was acceptable without its Coltranes and Shorters, it was at its strongest with Davis firmly at its head and so it proved.

A superbly performed *My Man's Gone Now* was a reminder that Frederick Murphy had also been told that, 'You don't play 1955 music or that straight crap like *My Funny Valentine*, (now)'. If there was one man whose playing shrieked that improvised music was about 'how' and not 'what' it was Davis and on *Man's Gone* his playing was majestic proof that any material was acceptable. He remained economical in his realistion of it, he remained part of the textural whole as befitted the electric band: but here was the unpredictable man making it difficult for listeners to pre-plan his route.

In the following year Lee Jeske reported (*Jazz Journal International*, November 1982) another phenomenon, Miles Davis the bon vivant. At New York's Jones Beach Festival, 'he was in ebullient spirits, mugging to the audience, twice stepping up to an unattended mike pretending to be about to sing, grinning and prancing; and then playing two full one-hour sets'. Sadly the American critic goes on to say that the band still left much to be desired and that he had heard Davis play better on many occasions.

Miles was getting stronger, however, and, even if performances were patchy, good notices were becoming more frequent. Jeske himself reported catching the band in far better shape early in 1983 and, more significantly, that Davis had recruited the talented John Scofield. The arrival of the Ohio guitarist was at Bill Evans's suggestion and, at first, merely doubled the feature guitar roster. Both Scofield and Mike Stern played at the London concert in April and with Davis in good humour and good lip, the band more than deserved its favourable audience reaction.

High energy funk and rock rhythms remained the basis of the music but Davis was approaching his own role within the band in a more studied way, cognizant of what had gone before. There was the paradox of him taking advantage of studio facilities by pre-recording organ parts and splicing them in later (*Star People*), and then appeasing his own love of the extempore by ignoring studio gadgetry and playing an insistent keyboard vamp with one hand and crackling trumpet with the other.

Despite its fashionable aspects, some of Davis's eighties music could be judged as as act of atavism. He was again looking at adaptations of the twelve bar form, although blues performances, the ultimate return to long distanced roots, tended to offer more to the B.B. King-style solos by Stern and musically cosmopolitan dialogues by Scofield. Davis, always a good blues player, was keeping it simple, however, and in the heartfelt trumpet parts he was saying no to the concept of rock as a description of his music.

His was unequivocally black music and it was perhaps appropriate that the Black Music Association should throw a press party at New York's Radio City late in the year. There was still evidence that, although playing with more strength and conviction with every concert or record date, CBS were still struggling for issuable material. Used to being fed timeless near masterpieces for the first ten years of their association had led them to expect nothing less. In fact, Davis had by the early eighties began to flirt with the synthesizer and there were three tracks on *Decoy* that had very little trumpet and no solos at all. It was, however, one of the best of the revivalist Davis records and used elements of dissonance to colour the overall sound of the band. It was certainly Scofield's best contribution on record and Branford Marsalis offered some very fine saxophone parts.

Nevertheless, one cannot help but wonder why *Robot 415* was included at all. It runs for a bare one minute and, just as Davis commences his solo, it is faded out. The inclusion of such items does suggest novelty appeal and infers that jingles are acceptable if 'catchy' enough.

Perhaps the jazz world must accept Davis as its most truly enigmatic character. At London's 1984 Capital Festival, further evidence was offered as he treated two performances on the same evening in a strangely cavalier manner. For the first 'house', he came on late and then used the set as little more than a warm-up for the second. After the interval, he played with an authority and grace missing so often in the recent past.

Bob Berg, a replacement for Marsalis, played orthodox saxophone in the Shorter manner and, with Scofield now in complete accord with the music, Davis had a group as integrated as any since 'Bitches Brew'. It was Davis who made the major score, however, delving into his blues heritage at one moment, soaring into lightly cascading runs the next. The bell of his trumpet, as usual, pointed toward the floor but his spirit was high and there was not one solo interlude that did not set out to be a creative entity.

Once again, a Miles Davis come back had become a fait accompli and, in December 1984, his credibility was again established on his terms. In that month he went to Copenhagen and there received the Leonie Sonning Music Foundation Prize for the year. Danish composer and trumpeter Palle Mikkelborg wrote a piece in his honour and it was performed by twenty seven musicians. Davis himself played a long solo and later asked Mikkelborg to arrange for the recording of the work.

Davis' public image was generally more outgoing and this was an attitude that he carried over into 1985. Concerts found him moving toward the professional photographers in the front row, only to block their lenses with the bell of his horn. He would then 'skip' to side stage, pose for the amateurs and treat the whole process as a joke.

His musical involvement was unimpaired and his more approach-able attitude brought favourable audience response. More than twelve thousand watched each of his two Nice Festival appearances and, at the Dutch, North Sea extravaganza, he opened two hours earlier to provide an extra set. He played well in London's Capital Jazz Week and only at New York's Kool event did he draw more reserved notices.

A record drawn from 1984 and 1985 sources documented his progress and *Something's On Your Mind* offered a Davis presenting the funk language with all of his old authority. Disappointingly, Berg was featured somewhat less than usual but this was due to Davis' changed approach to his studio dates. He no longer thought of individual 'takes', a great deal of material was recorded and it was later edited to issuable proportions. The resulting musical précis usually offered the best music available but it did give an unbalanced picture of the total session.

In 1986, changes in the Davis band continued to occur. Berg

remained a stalwart but the now clearly defined guitar role was taken over by the young Robben Ford. He proved to be more than equal to the challenge and Davis again played well on the festival circuit.

A change of record company came during the year but the move to Warner Brothers was not an immediate success. *TuTu*, the first release, was distinctly disappointing, with Davis cast as 'product', his trumpet parts anonymous and, despite the presence of guests such as drummer George Duke and violinist Michael Urbaniak, the overall impression was one of commercial awareness.

Such aesthetic stumblings were becoming a frequent part of the Davis career curve but his ability to bounce back was equally certain. His position as one of jazz music's most outstanding figures was not in doubt. Sycophants had seen him walk on water but, on many occasions, he had been in the vanguard of the music's developments. His flirtation with funk/rock had been largely successful and his current (1988) band has few peers.

It could productively be argued that, since the late sixties, he has followed a route that leaves the jazz mainstream. This is a matter of complete indifference to him and the all important consideration is that Miles Davis, master jazz musician, can call his music what he likes. In terms of creativity, passion and innovatory inspiration, he has had few rivals and there are enough 'indispensible' records in the catalogue to provide irrefutable proof of his genius. Without *Kind Of Blue* and *Sketches Of Spain* the whole world would have been a sadder place.

Bibliography

1 *These Jazzmen Of Our Time* by Charles Fox, Raymond Horricks and Alun Morgan (Gollancz)
2 *Such Sweet Thunder* by Whitney Balliett (Macdonald)
3 *Jazz on Record* by Alun Morgan (Hanover Books)
4 *Chasing the Trane* by J.C. Thomas (Elm Tree books)
5 *Miles Davis* by Ian Carr (Paladin)
6 *John Coltrane* by Bill Cole (Schirmer Books)
7 *Jazz Lives* by Michael Ullman (Perigree Books)
8 *Illustrated Encyclopedia of Jazz* by Brian Case and Stan Britt (Salamander Books)
9 *Encyclopedia of Jazz In the Seventies* by Leonard Feather and Ira Gitler (Quartet Books)
10 *Bird Lives* by Ross Russell (Quartet Books)
   Modern Jazz by Alun Morgan and Raymond Horricks (Gollancz)
   As Serious As Your Life by Valerie Wilmer (Allison and Busby)

With special thanks to Dave Driver and Graham Fowler for the use of their record collections.

Selected Discography

I have based my selections on recordings mentioned in the text and on those generally available at the time of going to press.

The following abbreviations have been used: (Am) United States of America; (arr) arrangement; (as) alto sax; (b) bass; (bars) baritone sax; (bcl) bass clarinet; (cond) conductor; (d) drums; (elb) electric bass; (elp) electric piano; (etp) electric trumpet; (Eu) Europe; (flh) flugel horn; (flu) flute; (frh) french horn; (g) guitar; (LA) Los Angeles; (NYC) New York City; (org) organ; (p) piano; (per) percussion; (SF) San Francisco; (sop) soprano sax; (tb) trombone; (tp) trumpet; (ts) tenor sax; (tu) tuba; (vbs) vibraphone; (vcl) vocal; (vtb) valve trombone.

TONY MIDDLETON, *London*, August 1987

Non Miles Davis Recordings mentioned in the text

CLAUDE THORNHILL AND HIS ORCHESTRA
Louis Mucci, Ed Zandy, Red Rodney (tp); Allan Langstaff, Tak Takvorian (tb); Sandy Siegelstein, Walter Welscher (frh); James Gemus, Vic Harris (cl); Danny Polo, Lee Konitz, Micky Folus, Mario Rollo, Bill Bushey (reeds); Claude Thornhill (p, arr); Bill Barber (tu); Barry Gailbraith (g); Joe Schulman (b); Billy Exner (d); Gil Evans, Gerry Mulligan, Bill Borden, Rusty Dedrick, John Hefti (arr).

SNOWFALL/ROBBINS' NEST/CABIN IN THE SKY/'DEED I DO/HAPPY STRANGER/
MEDLEY/JUST ABOUT THIS TIME LAST NIGHT/DONNA LEE/POOR LITTLE RICH GIRL/
POLKA DOTS AND MOONBEAMS/I MAY BE WRONG/ADIOS/SOMETIMES I'M HAPPY/
PUTTIN' AND TAKIN'/SUNDAY DRIVIN'/ANTHROPOLOGY

HINDSIGHT (Eu) HSR 108

Title: *The uncollected Claude Thornhill*

CHARLES MINGUS JAZZ WORKSHOP

Jimmy Knepper, Willie Dennis (tb); Jackie McLean, John Handy (as);
Booker Ervin (ts); Pepper Adams (bars); Mal Waldron (p) −1; Horace
Parlan (p); Charles Mingus (b); Dannie Richmond (d).

NYC. February 4, 1959

E'S FLAT, AH'S FLAT TOO −1/MY JELLY ROLL SOUL/TENSIONS/MOANIN'/CRYIN'
BLUES/WEDNESDAY NIGHT PRAYER MEETING

ATLANTIC (Am) SD1305

Title: *Blues and roots*

CHARLES MINGUS JAZZ WORKSHOP

Richard Williams (tp); Jimmy Knepper (tb); John Handy (as); Booker Ervin,
Benny Golson (ts); Jerome Richardson (bars, flu); Teddy Charles (vbs);
Roland Hanna (p) −1; Nico Bunink (p) −2; Charles Mingus (b); Danny
Richmond (d).

NYC. November 1, 1959

GUNSLINGING BIRD −1/SONG WITH ORANGE −1/DIANE −1/ FAR WELLS MILL
VALLEY/NEW NOW, KNOW HOW−2
(omit Teddy Charles).

Don Ellis (tp); Jimmy Knepper (tb); John Handy (as); Booker Ervin, Benny
Golson (ts); Roland Hanna (p); Maurice Brown, Seymour Barab (cello) −1;
Charles Mingus (b); Danny Richmond (d).

NYC, November 13, 1959

SLOP/PUT ME IN THAT DUNGEON −1/MOOD INDIGO/THINGS 'AINT WHAT THEY
USED TO BE

COLUMBIA (Am) CL1440, CBS (Eu) 21101

Title: *Mingus Dynasty*

HERBIE HANCOCK QUINTET

Freddie Hubbard (tp, flh); Dexter Gordon (ts); Herbie Hancock (p); Butch
Warren (b); Billy Higgins (d).

NYC. May 28, 1962

WATERMELON MAN/THREE BAGS FULL/EMPTY POCKETS/THE MAZE/DRIFTIN'/
ALONE AND I

BLUE NOTE (Eu) BST 84109

Title: *Takin' off*

Miles Davis – Selected Discography

Miles Davis SAVOY studio recordings with Charlie Parker issued by RCA Europe in five volumes: Savoy WL70520, 70527, 70548, 70813, 70832.

Miles Davis DIAL studio recordings with Charlie Parker issued by Spotlite: 101, 104,105,106.

MILES DAVIS ORCHESTRA

Miles Davis (tp); Mike Zwerin (tb); Junior Collins (frh); Bill Barber (tu); Lee Konitz (as); Gerry Mulligan (bars, arr –1); John Lewis (p, arr –2); Al McKibbon (b); Max Roach (d); Gil Evans (arr –3); Kenny Hagood (vcl –4); Symphony Sid (mc).

Broadcast from Royal Roost, NYC, September 4, 1948
MOVE –2/WHY DO I LOVE YOU –1,4/GODCHILD –1/S'IL VOUS PLAIT –2/MOON DREAMS –3/HALLUCINATIONS –2

DURIUM-CICALA (Eu) BJL 8003

MILES DAVIS ORCHESTRA

As for Sept 4, 1948 except Kai Winding (tb), Al Haig (p), Joe Schulman (b) replace Zwerin, Lewis and McKibbon.

		NYC, January, 21, 1949
3395–3	JERU –1	CAPITOL (Eu) CAPS 1024
3396–3	MOVE –2	"
3397–2	GODCHILD –1	"
3398–1	BUDO –2	"

As for Sept 4, 1948 except J.J. Johnson (tb), Sandy Siegelstein (frh), Nelson Boyd (b), Kenny Clarke (d) replace Zwerin, Collins, McKibbon and Roach. Add John Carisi (arr-5).

		NYC, April 22, 1949
3764	VENUS DE MILO –1	CAPITOL (Eu) CAPS 1024
3765	ROUGE –2	"
3766–2	BOPLICITY –3	"
3767–2	ISRAEL –5	"

As for Sept 4, 1948 except J.J. Johnson (tb), Gunther Schuller (frh) replace Zwerin and Collins

		NYC, March 9, 1950
4346	DECEPTION	CAPITOL (Eu) CAPS 1024
4347	ROCKER –1	"
4348	MOON DREAMS	"

MILES DAVIS BAND
Miles Davis (tp); Benny Green (tb); Sonny Rollins (ts); John Lewis (p); Percy Heath (b); Roy Haynes (d).

f5NYC, January 17, 1951
PRESTIGE (Eu) PR24054

128A	MORPHEUS	
129B	DOWN	"
130A	BLUE ROOM	"
130B	BLUE ROOM	"
131B	WHISPERING	"

LEE KONITZ SEXTET
Miles Davis (tp); Lee Konitz (as); Sal Mosca (p); Billy Bauer (g); Arnold Fishkin (b); Max Roach (d).

NYC, March 8, 1951
PRESTIGE (AM) 7827

140B	ODJENAR	
141B	EZZ-THETIC	"
142B	HI BECK	"
143B	YESTERDAYS—1	"
	1— Max Roach out on this track	

Title: *Ezz-thetic*

MILES DAVIS ALL STARS
Miles Davis (tp); Jackie McLean (as); Sonny Rollins (ts); Walter Bishop (p); Tommy Potter (b); Art Blakey (d).

NYC, October 5, 1951
PRESTIGE (Eu) PR24054

228	CONCEPTION	
229	OUT OF THE BLUE	"
230	DENIAL	"
321	BLUING	"
232	DIG	"
233	MY OLD FLAME	"
234	IT'S ONLY A PAPER MOON	"

MILES DAVIS BAND
Miles Davis (tp); Sonny Rollins, 'Charlie Chan'/Charlie Parker (ts); Walter Bishop (p); Percy Heath (b); Philly Joe Jones (d).

NYC, January 30, 1953
ORIGINAL JAZZ CLASSICS (Am) OJC071

450	COMPULSION	
451–1	SERPENT'S TOOTH	"
451–2	SERPENT'S TOOTH	"
452	ROUND MIDNIGHT	"

MILES DAVIS ALL STARS
Miles Davis (tp); Sonny Truitt (tb); Al Cohn, Zoot Sims (ts); John Lewis (p);
Leonard Gaskin (b); Kenny Clarke (d).

NYC, February 19, 1953

423	TASTY PUDDING	PRESTIGE (Eu) PR24054
424	WILLIE THE WAILER	"
425	FLOPPY	"
426	FOR ADULTS ONLY	"

MILES DAVIS QUARTET
Miles Davis (tp); John Lewis (p); Percy Heath (b); Max Roach (d).

NYC, May 19, 1953

479	WHEN LIGHTS ARE LOW	PRESTIGE (Eu) PR24077
480	TUNE UP	"

MILES DAVIS QUARTET
Miles Davis (tp); Horace Silver (p); Percy Heath (b); Art Blakey (d).

New Jersey, March 6, 1954

WELL YOU NEEDN'T/LAZY SUSAN/WEIRDO/THE LEAP/TAKE-OFF/IT NEVER ENTERED
MY MIND
Blue Note (Am/Eu) BST81502 (Miles Davis Vol. 2).
Note: Vol. 1 BST 81501.

As for March 6, 1954.

NYC, March 15, 1954

556	FOUR	PRESTIGE (Eu) PR24077
557	OLD DEVIL MOON	"
558	BLUE HAZE PARTS 1 & 2	"

MILES DAVIS QUINTET
Miles Davis (tp); Dave Schildkraut (as); Horace Silver (p); Percy Heath (b);
Kenny Clarke (d).

New Jersey, April 3, 1954

559	SOLAR	PRESTIGE (Eu) PR24077
560	YOU DON'T KNOW WHAT LOVE IS —1	"
561	LOVE ME OR LEAVE ME	"
562	I'LL REMEMBER APRIL	"
	—1 omit Schildkraut.	

MILES DAVIS SEXTET
same except omit Schildkraut; add J.J. Johnson (tb); Lucky Thompson (ts).

New Jersey, April 29, 1954

568	BLUE'N'BOOGIE PARTS 1 & 2	PRESTIGE (Eu) PR24077
569	WALKIN' PARTS 1 & 2	"

MILES DAVIS QUINTET
same except omit Johnson and Thompson; add Sonny Rollins (ts).

New Jersey, June 29, 1954

| 592 | BUT NOT FOR ME | PRESTIGE (Eu) PR24077 |

MILES DAVIS SEXTET
Miles Davis (tp); Milt Jackson (vbs); Thelonious Monk (p); Percy Heath (b); Kenny Clarke (d).

New Jersey, December 24, 1954

| 676 | BAGS GROOVE | PRESTIGE (Eu) PR24077 |
| 679 | THE MAN I LOVE | " |

Note: *Swing Spring* mentioned in the text is from the above session. Issued on Prestige (Eu) 61158.

MILES DAVIS QUARTET
Miles Davis (tp); Red Garland (p); Oscar Pettiford (b); Philly Joe Jones (d).

New Jersey, June 7, 1955

745	I DIDN'T	ORIGINAL JAZZ CLASSICS (Am) OJC004
746	WILL YOU STILL BE MINE	"
747	GREEN HAZE	"
748	I SEE YOUR FACE BEFORE ME	"
749	NIGHT IN TUNISIA	"
750	A GAL IN CALICO	"

Title: *The Musings of Miles*

MILES DAVIS QUINTET
Miles Davis (tp); Britt Woodman (tb); Teddy Charles (vbs); Charles Mingus (b); Elvin Jones (d).

NYC, July 9, 1955

NATURE BOY/ALONE TOGETHER/THERE'S NO YOU/EASY LIVING
Original Jazz Classics (Am) OJCO43 (Blue Moods).

MILES DAVIS/MILT JACKSON
Miles Davis (tp); Jackie McLean (as) −1; Milt Jackson (vbs); Ray Bryant (p); Percy Heath (b); Art Taylor (d).

New Jersey, August 5, 1955

781	DR. JACKIE −1	ORIGINAL JAZZ CLASSICS (Am) OJC012
782	BITTY DITTY	"
783	MINOR MARCH −1	"
784	BLUES CHANGES	"

Title: *Miles Davis and Milt Jackson*

MILES DAVIS QUINTET
Miles Davis (tp); John Coltrane (ts); Red Garland (p); Paul Chambers (b); Philly Joe Jones (d).

NYC, October 27, 1955

| C054130 | AH-LEU-CHA | CBS (E) 88029 |

THE NEW MILES DAVIS QUINTET
As above

New Jersey, November 16, 1955

814	STABLEMATES	ORIGINAL JAZZ CLASSICS (Am) 0JC006
815	HOW AM I TO KNOW	"
816	JUST SQUEEZE ME	"
817	THERE IS NO GREATER LOVE −1	"
818	THE THEME	"
819	S'POSIN	"
	−1 omit Coltrane.	

Title: *Miles*

MILES DAVIS QUINTET
Miles Davis (tp); Sonny Rollins (ts); Tommy Flanagan (p); Paul Chambers (b); Art Taylor (d).

New Jersey, March 16, 1956

864	IN YOUR OWN SWEET WAY	ORIGINAL JAZZ CLASSICS (Am) 0JC071
865	NO LINE	"
866	VIERD BLUES	"

MILES DAVIS QUINTET
As for October 1955

New Jersey, May 11, 1956

888	IN YOUR OWN SWEET WAY	PRESTIGE (Eu) PR24034
889	DIANE	"
890	TRANE'S BLUES	"
891	SOMETHING I DREAMED LAST NIGHT	"
892	IT COULD HAPPEN TO YOU	PRESTIGE (Eu) 81105
893	WOODY'N YOU	"
894	AHMAD'S BLUES −1	PRESTIGE (Eu) PR 24034
895	THE SURREY WITH THE FRINGE ON TOP	"
896	IT NEVER ENTERED MY MIND	"
897	WHEN I FALL IN LOVE	"
898	SALT PEANUTS	"
899	FOUR	"
900	THE THEME 1	"
901	THE THEME 2	"

−1 features rhythm only. PR24034 = Workin' (PR7166) and Steamin' (PR 7200).
Other titles on 81105 from October 26, 1956.

As previously

C056090	DEAR OLD STOCKHOLM	CBS (Eu) 88029
C056091	BYE BYE BLACKBIRD	"
C056092	TADD'S DELIGHT	"

As above

NYC, September 10, 1956

C056584	ALL OF YOU	CBS (Eu) 88029
C056586	ROUND MIDNIGHT	"

As above

New Jersey, October 26, 1956

995	IF I WERE A BELL	ORIGINAL JAZZ CLASSICS (Am) 0JC190
996	WELL YOU NEEDN'T	"
997	ROUND MIDNIGHT	"
998	HALF NELSON	"
999	YOU'RE MY EVERYTHING	"
1000	I COULD WRITE A BOOK	"
1001	OLEO	ORIGINAL JAZZ CLASSICS (Am) OJC128
1002	AIREGIN	"
1003	TUNE UP	"
1004	WHEN LIGHTS ARE LOW	"
1005	BLUES BY FIVE	"
1006	MY FUNNY VALENTINE −1	"

MILES DAVIS with orchestra under the direction of GIL EVANS

Bernie Glow, Ernie Royal, Louis Mucci, Taft Jordan, John Carisi (tp); Frank Rehak, Jimmy Cleveland, Joe Bennett, Tom Mitchell (tb); Willie Ruff, Tony Miranda (frh); Bill Barber (tu); Lee Konitz (as); Romeo Penque, Sid Cooper (woodwinds); Danny Bank (bcl); Paul Chambers (b); Art Taylor (b); Miles Davis (flh); Gil Evans (arr).

NYC, May 6, 1957

C057917	THE MAIDS OF CADIZ	COLUMBIA (Am) CL1041, CBS (Eu) 62496
C057918	THE DUKE	" "

As above

NYC, May 10, 1957

C057933	MY SHIP	COLUMBIA (Am) CL1041, CBS (Eu) 62496
C057934	MILES AHEAD	" "

As above

NYC, May 23, 1957

C058017	NEW RHUMBA	COLUMBIA (Am) CL1041, CBS (Eu) 62496
C058018	BLUES FOR PABLO	"
C058019	SPRINGSVILLE	"

As previously

C058171   I DON'T WANNA BE KISSED   COLUMBIA (Am) CL1041,
                                             CBS (Eu) 62496

C058172   THE MEANING OF THE BLUES   "
58173   LAMENT   "

Note: On one or more of the above dates Jim Buffington (frh) and Eddie Caine (woodwinds) replace Tony Miranda and Sid Cooper.
Title: *Miles Ahead*

MILES DAVIS QUINTET
Miles Davis (tp); Barney Wilen (ts); Rene Urtreger (p); Pierre Michelot (b); Kenny Clarke (d).

WOODY'N YOU/BAG'S GROOVE/WHAT'S NEW?/BUT NOT FOR ME/FOUR
                                     CELLULOID (Eu) CEL 6745

As above
WALKIN'/WELL YOU NEEDN'T/'ROUND MIDNIGHT/LADY BIRD
                                     CELLULOID (Eu) CEL 6746
NOTE: THE ABOVE IS A DOUBLE LP: *The Complete Amsterdam Concert*

MILES DAVIS
Miles Davis (tp, flh −1); Cannonball Adderley (as); John Coltrane (ts); Red Garland (p); Paul Chambers (b); Philly Joe Jones (d).

C060199   TWO BASS HIT   COLUMBIA (Am) PC9428, CBS (Eu) 85553
C060201   STRAIGHT NO CHASER   "   "
C060202   MILESTONES −1   "   "
Note: One further title from this session by the rhythm section only.

As above

C060203   DR. JEKYLL   COLUMBIA (Am) PC9428, COLUMBIA 85553
C060204   SID'S AHEAD   "   "
Note: Red Garland does not play on the last title; Davis also plays piano.
Title: *Milestones*

MILES DAVIS with orchestra under the direction of GIL EVANS
Louis Mucci, Ernie Royal, Johnny Coles, Bernie Glow (tp); Jimmy
Cleveland, Joe Bennett, Frank Rehak, Dick Hixon (tb); Willie Ruff, Julius
Watkins, Gunther Schuller (frh); Bill Barber (tu); Cannonball Adderley (as);
Phil Bodner, Romeo Penque (fl); Danny Bank (bass cl); Paul Chambers (b);
Philly Joe Jones (d); Gil Evans (ar); Miles Davis (tp, flh −1).

NYC, July 22, 1958

C061300	MY MAN'S GONE NOW−1	COLUMBIA (Am) PC8085,
		CBS (Eu) 32188
C061301	GONE, GONE, GONE−2	"
C061302	GONE−1	"

As above except Jimmy Cobb (d) for Jones

NYC, July 29, 1958

C061359	HERE COMES DE HONEYMAN	COLUMBIA (Am) PC8085,
		CBS(Eu)32188
C061360	BESS, YOU IS MY WOMAN NOW−1	"
C061361	IT AIN'T NECESSARILY SO−1	"
C061362	FISHERMAN, STRAWBERRY AND DEVIL CRAB−1	"

As above except Jerome Richardson (fl) for Bodner.

NYC, August 4, 1958

C061366	PRAYER−1	COLUMBIA (Am) PC8085, CBS (Eu) 32188
C061367	BESS, OH WHERE'S MY BESS−1	" "
X061368	THE BUZZARD SONG−1	" "

As above

NYC, August 18, 1958

C061421	SUMMERTIME	COLUMBIA (Am) PC8085, CBS (Eu) 32188
C061422	THERE'S A BOAT THAT'S LEAVING SOON−1	" "
C061423	I LOVES YOU PORGY	" "

Title: *Porgy and Bess*

MILES DAVIS SEXTET
Miles Davis (tp); Cannonball Adderley (as); John Coltrane (ts); Wynton Kelly
(p); Paul Chambers (b); Jimmy Cobb (d).

NYC, March 2, 1959

C062290	FREDDIE FREELOADER	COLUMBIA (Am) CS8163,
		CBS (Eu) 62066
C062291	SO WHAT−1	"
C062292	BLUE IN GREEN−1	"

Note: Adderley does not play on the last title; Bill Evans (p) −1 replaces
Kelly.

As previously

NYC, April 22, 1959
C062293 FLAMENCO SKETCHES COLUMBIA (Am) CS8163,
CBS (Eu) 62066

C062294 ALL BLUES "
Title: *Kind of Blue*

MILES DAVIS with orchestra conducted by GIL EVANS
Bernie Glow, Ernie Royal, Louis Mucci, Taft Jordan (tp); Frank Rehak, Dick
Hixon (tb); John Barrows, Jim Buffington, Earl Chapin (frh); Jay McAllister
(tu); Al Block, Ed Caine (flu); Harold Feldman (oboe, cl); Danny Bank (bass
cl); Janet Putman (harp); Paul Chambers (b); Jimmy Cobb (d); Elvin Jones
(per); Gil Evans (arr); Miles Davis (tp –1), flh –2).

NYC, November 20, 1959
C063791 CONCIERTO DE ARANJUEZ –1,2 COLUMBIA(Am)PC8271,
CBS(Eu)32023

As above except Johnny Coles (tp), Joe Singer, Tony Miranda (frh), Bill
Barber (tu), Romeo Penque (reeds), Jackie Knitzer (bassoon) replace Mucci,
Jordan, Barrows, Chapin, McAllister and Caine.

NYC, March 10, 1960
C064558 THE PAN PIPER –1 COLUMBIA (Am) PC8271, CBS (Eu) 32023

As above plus Louis Mucci (tp).

NYC, March 11, 1960
C064560 SOLEA –1 COLUMBIA (AM)PC8271, CBS (Eu) 32023
C064561 WILL O'THE WISP –1 " "
C064562 SAETA –1 " "
Title: *Sketches of/from Spain*

MILES DAVIS QUINTET
Miles Davis (t); John Coltrane (ts); Wynton Kelly (p); Paul Chambers (b);
Jimmy Cobb (d).

Stockholm, Sweden, March 22, 1960
SO WHAT/ON GREEN DOLPHIN STREET/ALL BLUES – THE THEME

DRAGON (Eu) DRLP90

SO WHAT/FRAN-DANCE/WALKIN' – THE THEME

DRAGON (Eu) DRLP91

Note: this is a double LP recorded in concert at the Konserthuset which also
included an interview with John Coltrane.
Title: *Live in Stockholm, 1960*

As previously except Sonny Stitt (as, ts) replaces Coltrane

Stockholm, Sweden, October 13, 1960

ON GREEN DOLPHIN STREET/'ROUND MIDNIGHT/THE THEME/ALL BLUES/THE THEME/ALL OF YOU

DRAGON (Eu) DRLP 129

WALKIN'/AUTUMN LEAVES/THE THEME/IF I WERE A BELL/ALL BLUES/THE THEME

DRAGON (Eu) DRLP 130

Note: this is a double LP record in concert at the Konserthuset.
Title: *Live in Stockholm, 1960*

As previous except Hank Mobley (ts) replaces Stitt.

NYC, March 7, 1961

C066235	DRAD-DOG	COLUMBIA (AM) CS8456, CBS (Eu) 62104	
C066236	PFRANCING	"	"

As above plus John Coltrane (ts) −1

NYC, March 20, 1961

C066500	SOME DAY MY PRINCE WILL COME −1	COLUMBIA (Am) CS8456, CBS (Eu) 62104	
C066501	OLD FOLKS	"	

As above except omit Mobley −2

NYC, March 21, 1961

C066505	TEO −1,2	COLUMBIA (Am) CS8456, CBS (Eu) 62104	
C066506	I THOUGHT ABOUT YOU	"	"

Title: *Some Day My Prince Will Come*

MILES DAVIS QUINTET

Miles Davis (tp); Hank Mobley (ts); Wynton Kelly (p); Paul Chambers (b); Jimmy Cobb (d).

SF, April 21, 1961

C067458	WALKIN'	COLUMBIA (Am) CS8469, CBS (Eu) 62306	
C067459	BYE BYE BLACKBIRD	"	"
C067460	ALL OF YOU	"	"
C067461	NO BLUES	"	"
C067462	BYE BYE (THEME)	"	"

Note: one further track from the above LP is a piano solo. LP title: *Miles Davis in Person: Friday night at the Blackhawk, San Francisco Vol 1*

As above

SF, April 22, 1961

C067464	WELL YOU NEEDN'T	COLUMBIA (Am) CS 8470, CBS (Eu) 62307	
C067465	FRAN-DANCE	"	"
C067466	SO WHAT	"	"
C067467	OLEO	"	"
C067468	IF I WERE A BELL	"	"
C067469	NEO	"	"

Title: *Miles Davis in Person: Saturday night at the Blackhawk, San Francisco Vol 2*

MILES DAVIS QUINTET with GIL EVANS AND HIS ORCHESTRA
Quintet: Miles Davis (tp); Hank Mobley (ts) −1; Wynton Kelly (p) −2; Paul Chambers (b); Jimmy Cobb (d). *Orchestra*: Bernie Glow, Ernie Royal, Louis Mucci, Johnny Coles (tp); Frank Rehak, Dick Hixon, Jimmy Knepper (tb); Julius Watkins, Paul Ingraham, Bob Swisshelm (frh); Bill Barber (tu); Jerome Richardson, Romeo Penque, Eddie Caine, Bob Tricario, Danny Bank (reeds, woodwinds); Janet Putman (harp); Bobby Rosengarden (per); Gil Evans (arr).

Carnegie Hall, NYC, May 19, 1961

C069842	SO WHAT −1,2	COLUMBIA (Am) PC8612, CBS (Eu) 85554	
C069843	SPRING IS HERE −2	"	"
C069844	NO BLUES −1,2	"	"
C069845	OLEO −1,2	"	"
C069846	SOME DAY MY PRINCE WILL COME −2	"	"
C069847	THE MEANING OF THE BLUES/LAMENT/	"	"
	NEW RHUMBA	"	"
	CONCIERTO DE ARANJUEZ	CBS (Eu) 460064.1	
	TEO	"	
	WALKIN'	"	
	I THOUGHT ABOUT YOU	"	

Note: Orchestra is not heard on C069844/5/6
Titles: *Miles Davis at Carnegie Hall* (PC8612, 85554)
    Live Miles: More Music from the Legendary Carnegie Hall Concert (460064.1)

MILES DAVIS with ORCHESTRA CONDUCTED BY GIL EVANS
Miles Davis (tp, flh −1); Orchestra same as May 19, 1961 except add Steve Lacey (sop).

NYC, July 27, 1962

C075683	CORCOVADO −2	COLUMBIA (Am) PC8906, CBS (Eu) 85556	
C075257	AOS PES DA CRUZ −2	"	"

As above

NYC, August 13, 1962

C075678	SONG NO. 1	COLUMBIA (Am) PC8906, CBS (Eu) 85556	
C075837	WAIT TILL YOU SEE HER	"	"

As above except Jimmy Buffington, John Barrows (frh); Elvin Jones (per) replace Ingraham, Swisshelm and Rosengarden.

NYC, November 6, 1962

C077119	ONCE UPON A SUMMERTIME	COLUMBIA (Am) PC8906, CBS (Eu) 85556
C077120	SONG NO.2	"

MILES DAVIS
Miles Davis (tp); Victor Feldman (p); Ron Carter (b); Frank Butler (d).

LA, April 16, 1963

HC071337	I FALL IN LOVE TOO EASILY	COLUMBIA (Am)CS8851, CBS (Eu) 62170
HC071338	BABY WON'T YOU PLEASE COME HOME	"
HC071339	BASIN STREET BLUES	"

As above; add George Coleman (ts)

LA, April 17, 1963

HC071342	SUMMER NIGHT	COLUMBIA (Am) PC8906, CBS (Eu) 85556

As above except Herbie Hancock (p), Tony Williams (d) replace Feldman and Butler.

NYC, May 14, 1963

C078342	SEVEN STEPS TO HEAVEN	COLUMBIA (Am) CS8851, CBS(Eu)62170
C078343	SO NEAR, SO FAR	"
C078872	JOSHUA	"

Title: *Seven Steps to Heaven*

As above

Juan-Les-Pins, France, July 26, 27, 29, 1963

C081817	AUTUMN LEAVES	COLUMBIA (Am) CS8983, CBS (Eu) 62390	
C081818	MILESTONES	"	"
C081819	JOSHUA	"	"
C081820	ALL OF YOU	"	"
C081821	WALKIN'	"	"

Title: *Miles Davis in Europe*

As for July 1963

NYC, February 12, 1964

C081836	SO WHAT	COLUMBIA (Am) CS9253, CBS (Eu) 62655	
C081838	WALKIN'	"	"
C081839	ALL OF YOU	COLUMBIA (AM) CS9106, CBS (Eu) 62510	
C081840	STELLA BY STARLIGHT	"	"
C081841	ALL BLUES	"	"
C081842	MY FUNNY VALENTINE	"	"
C081843	I THOUGHT ABOUT YOU	"	"
C088696	FOUR	COLUMBIA (Am) CS9253, CBS (Eu) 62655	
C088697	SEVEN STEPS TO HEAVEN	"	"
C088698	JOSHUA/GO-GO	"	"
C088699	THERE IS NO GREATER LOVE/GO-GO	"	"

As previously except Sam Rivers (ts) replaces Coleman.

Tokyo, Japan, July 14, 1964

IF I WERE A BELL/MY FUNNY VALENTINE/SO WHAT/WALKIN'/ALL OF YOU/THE THEME

As above except Wayne Shorter (ts) replaces Rivers.

Berlin, Germany, September 25, 1964

MILESTONES/AUTUMN LEAVES/SO WHAT/WALKIN'/THE THEME   CBS (Eu) 88626

Note: This is a double LP.
Title: *Miles Davis—Heard 'Round the World*

As above

LA, January 20, 1965

HC072230 E.S.P.	COLUMBIA (Am) CS9150, CBS (Eu) 85559	
HC072231 R.J.	„	„

As above

LA. January 21, 1965

HC077232 EIGHTY-ONE	COLUMBIA (Am) CS9150, CBS (Eu) 85559	
HC077233 LITTLE ONE	„	„

As above

LA January 22, 1965

HC072234 IRIS	COLUMBIA (Am) CS9150, CBS (Eu) 85559	
HC072235 AGITATION	„	„
HC072237 MOOD	„	„

Title: *E.S.P.*

As for January 1965

Plugged Nickle, Chicago, December 22, 1965

ROUND MIDNIGHT

As above

Plugged Nickle, Chicago, December 23, 1965

STELLA BY STARLIGHT/WALKIN'/AGITATION/GREEN DOLPHIN STREET/SO WHAT/
THE THEME/ALL BLUES/ YESTERDAYS/THE THEME   CBS (Eu) 88606

Note: This is a double LP
Title: *Live at the Plugged Nickle*

As for January 1965

NYC October 24 1966

C091173	CIRCLE	COLUMBIA (Am) CS9401, CBS (Eu) 85561	
C091174	ORBITS	„	„
C001175	DOLORES	„	„
C091176	FREEDOM JAZZ DANCE	„	„

87

As previously

NYC, October 25, 1966
| C091177 | GINGERBREAD BOY | COLUMBIA (Am) CS9401, CBS (Eu) 85561 |
| C091178 | FOOTPRINTS | " " |

Title: *Miles Smiles*

As above

NYC, May 16, 1967
| C093122 | LIMBO | COLUMBIA (Am) CS9532, CBS (Eu) 21143 |
| C093123 | VONETTE | " " |

As above

NYC, May 17, 1967
| C092211 | MASQUALERO | COLUMBIA (Am) CS9532, CBS (Eu) 21143 |
| C092212 | THE SORCERER | " " |

As above

NYC, May 24, 1967
| C092218 | PRINCE OF DARKNESS | COLUMBIA (Am) CS9532, CBS (Eu) 21143 |
| C092219 | PEE WEE | " |

Note: Miles Davis is not heard on 'Pee Wee'. One further title 'Nothing like you', from 1962 is also on this LP.
Title: *Sorcerer*

As for May 1967

NYC, June 7, 1967
| C092239 | NEFERTITI | COLUMBIA (Am) CS9594, CBS (Eu) 85551 |

As above

NYC, June 22, 1967
| C092250 | MADNESS | COLUMBIA (Am) CS9594, CBS (Eu) 85551 |

As above

NYC, June 23, 1967
| C092249 | HAND JIVE | COLUMBIA (Am) CS9594, CBS (Eu) 85551 |

As above

NYC, July 19, 1967
C092289	FALL	COLUMBIA (Am) CS9594, CBS (Eu) 85551
C092290	PINOCCHIO	" "
C092291	RIOT	" "

Title: *Nefertiti*

As previously, except add George Benson (g).

NYC, January 16, 1968

PARAPHERNALIA   COLUMBIA (Am) CS9628, CBS (Eu) 85548

Omit Benson

NYC, May 15, 1968

COUNTRY SON   COLUMBIA (Am) CS9628, CBS (Eu) 85548

As above

NYC, May 16, 1968

BLACK COMEDY   COLUMBIA (Am) CS9628, CBS (Eu) 85548

As above but Herbie Hancock plays elp

NYC, May 17, 1968

STUFF   COLUMBIA (Am) CS9628, CBS (Eu) 85548

Title: *Miles in the Sky*

MILES DAVIS

Miles Davis (tp); Wayne Shorter (ts); Herbie Hancock (elp); Ron Carter (elb); Tony Williams (d).

NYC, June 19, 1968

PETITS MACHINS   COLUMBIA (Am) CS9750, CBS (Eu) 63551

As above

NYC, June 20, 1968

TOUT DE SUITE   COLUMBIA (Am) CS9750, CBS (Eu) 63551

As above

NYC, June 21, 1968

FILLES DE KILIMANJARO   COLUMBIA (Am) CS9750,
CBS (Eu) 63551

As above, except Chick Corea (elp), Dave Holland (b) replace Hancock and Carter.

NYC, September 24, 1968

FRELON BRUN   COLUMBIA (Am) CS9750, CBS (Eu) 63551
MADEMOISELLE MABRY   COLUMBIA (Am) CS9750,
CBS (Eu) 63551

Title: *Filles de Kilimanjaro*

MILES DAVIS
Miles Davis (tp); Wayne Shorter (sop); Herbie Hancock, Chick Corea (elp);
Joe Zawinul (elp, org); John McLaughlin (g); Dave Holland (b); Tony
Williams (d).

NYC, February 18, 1969

SHHH/PEACEFUL/IN A SILENT WAY/IT'S ABOUT TIME   COLUMBIA (Am)
CS9875, CBS (Eu) 63630

Note: The above LP suffers much tape splicing/editing.
Title: *In a Silent Way*

MILES DAVIS
Miles Davis (tp, etp); Wayne Shorter (sop); Chick Corea (elp); Dave Holland
(b); Jack DeJohnette (d); Jim Riley, Charles Alias (per).

NYC, August 19, 1969

SANCTUARY   CBS (Eu) 66236

add Benny Maupin (bcl); Joe Zawinul (elp); John McLaughlin (g); Harvey
Brooks (elb); Lenny White (d).

same date

BITCHES BREW   CBS (Eu) 66236

add Larry Young (elp).

NYC, August 20, 1969

SPANISH KEY   CBS (Eu) 66236

Omit Joe Zawinul

same date

MILES RUNS THE VOODOO DOWN   CBS (Eu) 66236
Note: Miles Davis is not heard on other titles on this LP which were recorded
on the third day of the session (August 21).
Title: *Bitches Brew*

MILES DAVIS
Miles Davis (tp); Benny Maupin (bcl); Steve Grossman (sop); John
McLaughlin (elg); Herbie Hancock, Chick Corea (elp); Harvey Brooks (elb);
Ron Carter (b); Billy Cobham (d); Airto Moreira (per); Khalil Balakrishna
(electric sitar); Bihari Sharma (tamboura).

NYC, November 19, 1969

GREAT EXPECTATIONS/MULHER LARANJA   Columbia (Am) PG32866,
CBS (Eu) 88024

90

As previously, except Wayne Shorter (sop); Joe Zawinul (elp, farfisa), Dave Holland (b) replace Grossman, Hancock and Carter. Omit McLaughlin and Sharma. Add Jack DeJohnette (d).

NYC, January 27, 1970

LONELY FIRE   COLUMBIA (Am) PG32866, CBS (Eu) 88024

MILES DAVIS
Miles Davis (tp); Benny Maupin (bcl); Steve Grossman (sop); John McLaughlin (g); Dave Holland (elb); Jack DeJohnette (d).

NYC, March 30, 1970

GO AHEAD JOHN   COLUMBIA (Am) PG32866, CBS (Eu) 88024

MILES DAVIS
Miles Davis (tp); Steve Grossman (sop); Herbie Hancock (org); John McLaughlin (g); Mike Henderson (elb); Billy Cobham (d).

NYC, April 7, 1970

RIGHT OFF   COLUMBIA (Am) KC30455, CBS (Eu) 70089
YESTERNOW   "   "
Note: Brass/Synth/extra rhythm possibly added at a later date.
Title: *Jack Johnson* (Soundtrack)

MILES DAVIS
Miles Davis (tp); Steve Grossman (sop); Chick Corea (elp); Keith Jarrett (org); Dave Holland (elb); Jack DeJohnette (d); Airto Moreira (per).

Fillmore East, NYC, June 1970

WEDNESDAY MILES (June 17)/THURSDAY MILES (June 18)/FRIDAY MILES (June 19)/SATURDAY MILES (June 20).   COLUMBIA (Am) KG30038,
CBS (Eu) 66257

Note: The above is a double LP.
Title: *Live at Fillmore*

MILES DAVIS: LIVE EVIL
Miles Davis (tp); Wayne Shorter (sop, ts); Joe Zawinul, Chick Corea (keyboards); John McLaughlin (g); Dave Holland (b); Billy Cobham (d); Airto Moreira, Khalil Balakrishna (per).

NYC, February 6, 1970

MEDLEY: GEMINI/DOUBLE IMAGE

Miles Davis (tp); Steve Grossman (saxs); Herbie Hancock, Chick Corea, Keith Jarrett (keyboards); Ron Carter (b); Jack DeJohnette (d); Airto Moreira (per); Hermeto Pascoal (vcl).

NYC, June 3, 1970

NEM UM TALVEZ/SELIM

As previously, except add John McLaughlin (g); Dave Holland (b) replaces Carter. Hermeto Pascoal (elp, whistling).

NYC, June 7, 1970

LITTLE CHURCH

Miles Davis (tp); Gary Bartz (as); Keith Jarrett (p, elp); John McLaughlin (g); Michael Henderson (elb); Jack DeJohnette (d); Airto Moreira (per).

Washington, December 18, 1970

SIVAD/WHAT I SAY/FUNKY TONK/INAMORATA
Columbia (Am) KC30954, CBS (Eu) 67219

MILES DAVIS: ON THE CORNER
Miles Davis (tp); Benny Maupin (bcl); Dave Liebman (sop); Chick Corea, Herbie Hancock, Harold Williams (p, elp, synth); John McLaughlin (g); Colin Walcott (sitar); Michael Henderson (b); Jack DeJohnette (d); Billy Hart, Don Alias, M'tume (per); Badal Roy (tabla).

NYC, June 1, 1972

ON THE CORNER/NEW YORK GIRL/THINKIN' ONE THING/VOTE FOR MILES/BLACK SATIN

As above except Carlos Garnett (sop, ts) replaces Liebman.

NYC, June 6, 1972

ONE AND ONE/HELEN BUTTE/MR. FREEDOM X
Columbia (AM) KC31906, CBS (Eu) 85549.

MILES DAVIS: IN CONCERT
Miles Davis (tp); Carlos Garnett (sop); Cedric Lawson (keyboards); Reggie Lucas (g); Khalil Balakrishna (electric sitar); Mike Henderson (elb); Al Foster (d); M'tume (per) Badal Roy (tabla).

Philharmonic Hall, NYC, September 29, 1972

20.45/25.23/18.12/20.21.
Columbia (Am) KG32092, CBS (Eu) 68222

MILES DAVIS: GET UP WITH IT

NYC, September 1972

As for September 29, 1972
BILLY PRESTON/RATED X

Miles Davis (tp); unknown brass; Wade Marcus (arr/cond); Wally Chambers (harmonica); Cornell Dupree (g); Mike Henderson (elb); Al Foster, Bernard Purdie (d); M'tume (per); Billy Jackson (arr).

NYC, January 1973

RED CHINA BLUES

Miles Davis (tp, org); Dave Liebman (flu); John Stubblefield (sop); Reggie Lucas, Pete Cosey (g); Mike Henderson (elb); Al Foster (d); M'tume (per).

NYC, late 1973

CALYPSO FRELIMO

As above except omit Stubblefield; add Dominique Gaumont (g).

NYC, May 1974

HE LOVED HIM MADLY

As above, except Sonny Fortune (flu) replaces Liebman

NYC, June 1974

MAIYSHA

As above except omit Gaumont.

Same date

M'TUME
Columbia (Am) KG 33236, CBS (Eu) 88092

MILES DAVIS: THE MAN WITH THE HORN
Miles Davis (tp, elp); Randy Hall (voc, g, mini moog synthesizer, celeste); Robert Irving III (p, Yamaha CP 30); Felton Crews (b); Vincent Wilburn (d).

NYC, mid 1980

THE MAN WITH THE HORN

Miles Davis (tp, elp); Randy Hall (mini moog synthesizer); Robert Irving III (Yamaha CP 30); Felton Crews (b); Vincent Wilburn (d).

NYC mid 1980

SHOUT

Miles Davis (tp); Bill Evans (sop); Barry Finnerty (g) –1; Mike Stern (g) –2; Marcus Miller (elb); Al Foster (d); Sammy Figueroa (per).

NYC Spring 1981

BACK SEAT BETTY –1/ AIDA –1/URSULA –1/FAT TIME –2
Columbia (Am) PC36790, CBS (Eu) 84708

MILES DAVIS: WE WANT MILES
Miles Davis (tp, keyboards); Bill Evans (sop); Mike Stern (g); Marcus Miller (elb); Al Foster (d); Mino Cinelu (per).

Boston (June 27), NYC (July 5), Tokyo (Oct 4), 1981
JEAN-PIERRE (SHORT)/BACK SEAT BETTY/FAST TRACK/MY MAN'S GONE NOW/KIX
Columbia (Am) C2-38005, CBS (Eu) 88579

MILES DAVIS: STAR PEOPLE
Miles Davis (tp, keyboards); Bill Evans (sop, ts); Mike Stern, John Scofield (g); Marcus Miller, Tom Barney –1 (b); Al Foster (d); Mino Cinelu (per); Gil Evans (arr).

NYC 1983

COME AND GET IT/IT GETS BETTER/SPEAK –1/STAR PEOPLE/U'N'I/STAR ON CICELY
Columbia (Am) FC38657, CBS (Eu) 25395

MILES DAVIS: DECOY
Miles Davis (tp, synth); Branford Marsalis (sop); John Scofield (g); Darryl 'The Munch' Jones (b); Al Foster (d); Robert Irving III (synth, electric drum programming); Mino Cinelu (per).

1984

DECOY/CODE M.D./THAT'S RIGHT

Miles Davis (tp, synth); Mino Cinelu (per); Robert Irving III (synth, synth bass, electric drum programming).

1984

ROBOT 415

Miles Davis (synth); Darryl 'The Munch' Jones (b); Al Foster (d); Mino Cinelu (per).

NYC, 1984

FREAKY DEAKY

Miles Davis (tp, synth); Bill Evans (sop); John Scofield (g); Darryl 'The Munch' Jones (b); Al Foster (d)); Mino Cinelu (per).

Montreal, Canada, 1984

WHAT IS IT/THATS WHAT HAPPENED
Columbia (Am) FC 38991, CBS (Eu) 25951

MILES DAVIS: TUTU
Miles Davis (tp); Michael Urbaniak (electric violin) –1; Bernard Wright (Synth) –2; Paulinho Da Costa (perc) –3; Steve Reid (per) –4; Omar Hakim (d, per) –5; Marcus Miller (b, elb, sop, clarinets, synth); Jason Miles, Adam Holzman (synth programming); George Duke (misc instruments).

1986

TUTU –3/TOMAAS –2,5/PORTIA –3/SPLATCH –3,4/BACKYARD RITUAL –3/PERFECT WAY/DON'T LOSE YOUR MIND–1,2/FULL NELSON
Warner Brothers (Am) 25490-4, (Eu) 925 490-1

Miles Davis on Compact Disc

Ascenseur pour L'Echafaud	8225662 (IMS)
Cookin' with Miles Davis Quintet	FCD 6367094 (IMS)
Decoy	CD25951 (CBS)
Kind of Blue	CD62066 (CBS)
Man with the Horn	CD84708 (CBS)
Relaxin' with Miles	FCD 6277129 (IMS)
Sketches of Spain	CD 62327 (CBS)
Star People	CD 25395 (CBS)
Steamin' with Miles Davis Quintet	FCD6477166 (IMS)
TuTu	9254902 (WEA)
Under arrest	CD 26447 (CBS)
Workin' with Miles Davis Quintet	FCD 6477166 (IMS)

Distributors names are given in brackets.

LP titles not noted in the general discography:

BJL8003	Pre- Birth of the cool
CAPS1024	Birth of the cool
PR24054	Dig
PR24077	Tune up
OJC071	Collectors Items
88029	Miles Davis with John Coltrane
OJC128	Cookin'
OJC 190	Relaxin'
62655	Four and More
62510	My Funny Valentine
88024	Big Fun

Miles Davis Prestige recordings issued in U.S.A. 1980. Title: Miles Davis Chronicle: The Complete Prestige Recordings   PRESTIGE (Am) P012

Note: this set was a limited edition.